Handbook for the Amateur Paranormal Investigator or Ghost Hunter

How to Become a Successful Paranormal Group.

By Brian D. Parsons

Copyright © 2008
Brian D. Parsons

All rights reserved. No part of this work may be reproduced or transmitted in any form by any means electrical or mechanical, including photocopying, recording or translating into another language, or by any information storage or retrieval system, without written permission from the author.

Printed by Lulu, published by Brian D. Parsons, Solon, Ohio.

O.P.I.N. Books™ 2008.

ISBN- 978-0-6152-1271-5

Dedication

My first book is dedicated to my wife, Amy, who has patiently stood by my side throughout my obsession with this field and with this book. I would also like to thank her for taking her time to help me by editing my work.

I would like to thank those who said I should write about my thoughts and experiences and told me that I should leave my mark. I've never viewed myself as an expert in this field, but hopefully my words will be an inspiration to someone out there.

Special thanks go to those who thought I would never attempt to do this.

Handbook for the Amateur Paranormal Investigator or Ghost Hunter: How to become a successful paranormal group.

Part I: Welcome to the World of Ghosts!

Introduction
Chapter 1: Evolution
Chapter 2: Parapsychology and other terminology
Chapter 3: What else do I need to know?
Chapter 4: The Reality

Part II Getting Started

Chapter 1: Education
Chapter 2: Starting Your Own Group
Chapter 3: Getting Investigators
Chapter 4: Getting Noticed
Chapter 5: Common Pitfalls

Part III Getting Involved - Conducting an Investigation or hunt

Chapter 1: Initial Contact
Chapter 2: Art of Interviewing
Chapter 3: Science of Investigation
Chapter 4: Conducting a Hunt
Chapter 5: The Follow-up
Chapter 6: The Tools

Part IV Resources

Chapter 1: The Scientific Method
Chapter 2: Recommended Books
Chapter 3: Terminology
Chapter 4: Further Information

Introduction

This book will hopefully become a guide for those who have an interest in starting their own paranormal group or who are contemplating getting into the world of ghost hunting. I have gathered my knowledge and experiences into making this short guide to creating and maintaining a successful group as well as being successful as an investigator. My road to this book has not always been an easy one (and is one I am still navigating). My successes have come at many failures I have endured throughout my twelve years actively involved in this field.

    My hope is that I can teach those through my mistakes and failures and pass on the things that have brought me to being successful in this field. Many people have different definitions of "success", especially when it comes to this field. For many it is becoming well known or popular, having your group in a newspaper or television show. For me, my success is measured in helping those around me. In particular, the clients who need my help that have no idea what is going on in their lives are my main focus. Gathering evidence and my desire to gain knowledge of this field through these cases takes a back seat to helping those who merely want to stop or understand what is happening to them.

The biggest concern in recent years has been the continuing influx of paranormal groups. Television has been a major influence on how groups approach this field, but the surge in groups has been happening long before shows about ghosts or ghost hunting became mainstream. Along with this influx came misunderstanding, misinterpretation and many opinions that morphed into facts.

This is not to say that groups ten years ago were better than today's, but the knowledge that was handed down has been tainted by those who had little investment beyond personal glory and much has been lost due to lack of communication and other political problems.

I have been bothered by the decay of knowledge and approach for years. I hoped that things would change and the focus on this field would ebb, but I now realize that this field will continue to grow and the problems that have been seeded in this field will continue to blossom as well.

This book is my way of reaching out to potential and new groups (and hopefully established ones as well) to shed some light on this subject and put a little reality in with has become partially fictionalized over the years. My intent is to give newbies a chance to be successful without having to imitate other groups or television.

Part I: Welcome to the World of Ghosts!

Chapter 1: Evolution

I'll begin with a bit of background on ghost research past and present. When we think about "ghost hunting", we think of the television shows and think it's a relatively new pursuit. The ghost hunting movement actually began back in the mid 1800s. A European children's book author, Catherine Crowe, published a book, *The Night Side of Nature,* based on stories and accounts of ghosts. She was the first to use the German word "poltergeist" in print. There was also a stirring in the United States thanks to a couple of young girls known as the Fox sisters. This was a catalyst in the birth of the Spiritualist movement in the United States. Their fame officially began when Maggie and Kate Fox of Hydesville, New York, were purportedly able to communicate with a spirit of a deceased man who was supposedly buried on their property. The particulars of this individual case have been argued over the years as well as the validity of the abilities of the sisters.

This sparked others to gain heavy interest in communicating with the other side as Mediums began to spring up in New York and soon all over the United States. Also, during this time spirit photographs began to appear, a majority of which were fakes and frauds (my how history repeats itself). The popularity of this new fad also began to attract those who held little belief in the abilities of the Mediums and other individuals who were capitalizing on it. Harry Houdini, the famous magician, took part in uncovering how some of these individuals acted out their cons with their séance's, table-tipping and other illusions. This popularity lead to groups being formed to get to the bottom of the search for life after death.

The Society for Psychical Research (SPR) was officially created on February 20, 1882 in England. This new organization was formed from Cambridge University students and other individuals who had ties to possible paranormal situations as well as many skeptics who wanted to uncover the logic behind what was happening. The goal of the SPR was to investigate claims of parapsychological (psychic) phenomenon through objective investigation. Psychical research is the forefather of parapsychology (the branch of science that studies psychic or paranormal behavior). The United States formed its own Psychical research branch, the American Society of Psychical Research (ASPR) in 1885. These two organizations still exist to this day as well as a handful of others that have been born along the way (see Paranormal Association, Rhine Research Center, Parapsychology Foundation, Inc.).

This research has managed to stay popular with many fringe scientists over the years even though funding for psychical research had been cut dramatically in the 1970s and 1980s, due to the shift from mental to medical sciences. Mainstream science has no respect for Parapsychology for a variety of reasons. A lack of repeatability of experiments and most notably since there has not been much in the way of advancements or discoveries in the field in the last Century. Parapsychologists have managed to continue to study the field by specializing in other fields in close relation to Para-science, such as Psychology (to put food on the table). Somewhere in the last twenty years it has become increasingly popular for non-scientists (or what one would call amateurs) to pursue similar interests as the Parapsychologists, though the main focus has been on the survival of bodily death.

Refer to "Ghost Hunters: William James and the Search for Scientific Proof of Life After Death" for more information on the beginning of the ASPR as well as more into the story of the Fox sisters. See list of books in the back.

Chapter 2: Parapsychology and other Terminology

In this chapter we will discuss our parent field, parapsychology, as well as terminology used in ghost hunting and paranormal investigation. In order for the terminology to fall into place we will first discuss parapsychology, but let's quickly clear up a couple of definitions.

What's the difference between a ghost hunter and a paranormal investigator? These two terms actually mean two different things, though many in the field will argue this point. A ghost hunter is one who is merely in search of a ghost based upon a hunch or stories that a place is haunted. They also search cemeteries and abandoned buildings in hopes of experiencing or documenting a ghost or other paranormal activity. This category includes those who do this as a weekend pursuit or hobby and may or may not help clients. The critical difference is typically a lack of first-hand witnesses, a minimal pursuit to investigate the connections, validity, proper methods of scientific approach and appropriately rendering a true definition of what is taking place.

Helping clients is when a ghost hunter actually begins to cross the line as a paranormal investigator. A paranormal investigator is one who follows up on first hand accounts of paranormal activity and is attempting to create a controlled setting to conduct research into the actual events. The paranormal investigators are concerned with the connection of the client and their experiences and are not focused on having their own experiences (though it is icing on the cake). Unfortunately, the line between these two types of pursuits has been blurred over the years.

A reason for this is the use of technology. Groups think that by applying tools they are applying science and are conducting an investigation. If there are no current witnesses to any events you really are not investigating anything, but rather *searching or hunting* for something. This has really become confusing since the television show named after the pursuit has created a generation of loose cannons. The show is aptly named. The group comes in from hearing stories and set out to capture or record events. Even though they are using technology they are in search of their own experiences and typically do not involve the client in the so-called "investigation". They have separated the client from the experience and are not inclined to find a reason for that connection (which is actually the paranormal part, not the ghost itself).

Another set of terms that should be brought up are evidence and proof. For some odd reason some people stumble over these words or their concepts. Evidence displays a possibility about something, while proof establishes a conclusive truth based upon several pieces of evidence. A photograph of something that could be a ghost would constitute evidence, not proof. Photographs, videos and even electronic voice phenomena are documentation and can potentially be evidence, but none of these alone can constitute as proof, unless they are backing up an event as the documentation is captured.

Let's get back to parapsychology. The field is generally ignored by many ghost hunters as well as paranormal investigators for a variety of reasons. First, I just don't think they take the time to dig deep enough into ghosts to realize where they were first researched. Second, ghost hunters view the ghost as a ghost existing on its own while a Parapsychologist studies the connection of the living and the dead to interpret how a ghost exists from the living point of view (though they are interested in the ghost, it is not their main focus).

Hopefully, you will find this field a key to your

investigating as well as a map to help you understand how these events tie in to dealing with ghosts and their living companions.

As was stated in the first chapter, Parapsychology is the scientific study of psychic phenomena. So, what exactly are psychic phenomena? Most people might say it is mind reading or telling the future, well you're partly right. Parapsychology is simply cut into three distinct sections; extra sensory perception (ESP), Psychokinesis (PK) and survival of bodily death (ghosts, hauntings, etc.).

1. Extra Sensory Perception (ESP) - This is simply the ability to gain knowledge through means other than the five physical senses or by logical inference. It is the receptive side of the psychic world (the information is received from the outside world). ESP is broken down into three types.

A.) Telepathy- An awareness of information or emotions that exists in the mind of another person. Though we think of this as reading someone's mind, it is more like a willing transfer of thoughts or emotions.

B.) Clairvoyance- The ability to receive information from objects or events at the present time without the use of "normal" senses or by putting it together by obvious clues. This is visual information. There is also sound information "clairaudience", or physical sensations "clairsentience". Note that this is information in the present time and not past or future events.

      a.) Psychometry- A sub-category of clairvoyance where there is an ability to "read" the history of an object or location (or gain information about the people associated with it). This is one possible explanation for hauntings. Material objects or locations may somehow be able to record information in the electromagnetic field or other means.

      C.) Precognition- Receiving information about objects or events that exist in some future time. While clairvoyance simply crosses distance or space, precognition crosses space as well as time. This raises some eyebrows at how we think about reality and dimensions and would force science to do a lot of rewriting in the future.

      a.) Retrocognition- An awareness of objects and events that existed in the past. This may provide an alternate explanation to psychometry and hauntings. Instead of "reading" the history of an object or location from its electromagnetic field, the person receiving the information may simply be using that object or location as a position to look back at the past.

2.) Psychokinesis (PK) - This is the expressive side of psychic phenomena, "mind over matter".
      A.) Telekinesis - The ability to move an object from a distance. Many Parapsychologists have given up this term and simply use psychokinesis.

B.) Teleportation- The movement of an object from one location to another without its having traveled the distance between them. Basically, an object seemingly disappears from one spot and reappears in another (think Star Trek transporter). It's here where we can put ghost photographs and photos changed by psychics, as well as electronic voice phenomena (EVP).

C.) Poltergeist- Parapsychologists link the experience to a living person (agent) and to a stress related situation. Typically it has been said it surrounds a pre-teen or teenage female, though this is not always the case. Objects seem to move on their own power and apparitions may appear (seemingly attracted by the psychic activity). The activity is generally surrounding the agent. Many amateur ghost hunters feel that poltergeists are actually a type of ghost and do not associate them with the living, due to the behavior, but parapsychologists feel this is merely a side effect of the PK.

3.) Survival of Bodily Death- Now we're talking about ghosts. Survival of bodily death does not mean that the person is living, just that a recognizable and interactive aspect has carried on from that person beyond death. Some may call this the consciousness, soul or aura, but most agree it is some type of energy that continues to somehow exist outside the body. You'll notice that the following terminology may differ from what you may read elsewhere. I have adopted the most basic terms from Parapsychology; though others exist (I'll do my best to explain this along the way).

A.) Apparitions- This is what is seen, heard, felt or even smelled and is the remnant of the human personality that has somehow carried on after the death of the living body.

This is most often used as a synonym to the word ghost and many groups use apparition to describe a visual ghost, but parapsychologists use the word to describe the overall events that accompany them. Many amateur groups will use intelligent haunting to describe apparitional events. This does makes sense since an apparition seems to show some intelligence with its existence and it will interact with the living to differing degrees.

An apparition (when we see it) will appear as a regular human with regular proportions. Many skeptics will argue that if the "soul" can carry on beyond death, then how do clothes and other objects which have no mind to carry over appear? This is because; this is what the person wants you to see. Let's try an experiment. Close you eyes and imagine what you look like for a moment. Did you put clothes on yourself? Maybe you are wearing your favorite clothes or your most comfortable? This is what you would look like as a ghost. This is why ghosts do not appear nude, but rather as a reflection of what the person looked like during their life. This is how ESP fits into the world of ghosts. The information is sent between the living and the afterlife and it is this connection that parapsychologists are studying. It is commonly thought that many apparitions will appear without their feet or legs.

There have been certain cases where a child and adult ghost was actually the same ghost. An apparition can sometimes appear at different periods of their life and clothing may also change. This does beg the question: can ghosts appear however they want? The answer is that they might, but typically appear as what they did when they were alive and they do not seem to have that much control as to what they look like to the living.

Apparitions will seemingly carry on the personality of the living person they once were. If they were happy in life they may extend this feeling to the other side. Those who would interact with this apparition would share this feeling. The same would hold true if the apparition were a sad or even an angry person. Apparitions will also carry a seemingly physical part of them as well. If the person had a favorite scent this may be picked up by the living. It is not unusual to smell perfume, cigars or other smells associated with them in life at a haunted site when the apparition is present.

Apparitions of the living may also occur. A *crisis apparition* is an apparition of a dead (12 hours or less) or dying person as viewed by the living typically with someone who is close with that person. These are usually a one time occurrence and are generally connected to a time of death of the person appearing as the apparition. This may also take place as a phone call or even an instant message from the internet. It is a final communication before their physical death. These crisis apparitions have been known to carry on conversations and appear to be the person in full form.

Apparitions of the living that are not related with a dying process are called an out of body experience (OBE). A "part" of the mind leaves the body and may be visible to others and may even interact. Near Death Experience (NDE) describes when a person "leaves their body" during the process of dying. They obviously are able to come back to life to explain what they have witnessed. A few modern medicine procedures actually put the body in a position where it is brain dead to carry out certain surgical procedures. The patients or individuals who have experienced this process seem to describe it happening in the very same fashion, though science and skeptics argue over it having anything to do with consciousness surviving outside of the physical body.

B.) Hauntings- Hauntings refer to a location or object where activity is occurring, but without the intelligence that an apparitional event would have. These are often described as an event happening over and over like a broken record. This is a term that has been used in a dozen different ways with amateur groups as well as parapsychologists, so you may have seen this term used in a different way.

The easiest way to differentiate an apparition from a haunting is whether there is communication or an intelligence behind what is being experienced. A haunting has no intent on direct communication, though a person may perceive that the noises and events were communication through careful interviewing and investigation you can typically find evidence to support a haunting...

Imagine yourself confronted by a ghost. If the ghost looks at you or reacts to your presence or says your name it's probably an apparition. If it goes about its business despite your best efforts to communicate with it, you have a haunting.

Some will call a repetitive non-intelligent event a true haunting, then an apparitional event an intelligent haunting or apparitional haunting. They continue using the word haunting and attaching a prefix to describe varying ghost activity. Some use the word ghost to describe non-intelligent apparition and use haunting to describe an intelligent ghost. Confused yet? Whatever the term is used by any author or group there are two main descriptions; interactive and non-interactive. It is important to note now that we are not describing ghosts here, rather we are describing their affects on their surroundings or how they act by calling them apparitions or hauntings.

Chapter 3: What Else Do I Need to Know?

Now that we have discussed some of the terminology (and the problems that go along with them) we will now dive in to personal questions that you will need to answer as well as some insight you'll need to hear before you proceed too far into this field.

The first question you need to ask yourself before you get too far involved is: what are you looking for? Furthering this question, you will want to ask yourself other questions to truly discover your own motive for wanting to investigate this field. Are you in this because you had a previous encounter with something you thought was paranormal? Are you merely looking to have a paranormal experience? Are you doing this because you want to explore your "sensitive" or psychic side? Are you looking to provide "proof" of the paranormal or that ghosts really exist? Are you looking to become rich and/or famous from using this field as more than a hobby (writing books, being on television, being a professional parapsychologist, etc.)? These are the top reasons why many people get into this field. Unfortunately, most of them do not stay very long. Let's explore each path and why it may doom you to fall off the bandwagon.

You may have had a previous encounter and are now wondering, "Why?" or "How can I attempt to explain this"? I get a lot of people who want to join my group because of this personal pursuit of answers. There is nothing wrong with joining a group because of this, but you have to make this secondary to the group's vision. The pursuit of answers may not ever answer the personal ones that have happened to you, but may eventually provide you with insight to what may have happened to you.

Paranormal experience. Many people set out to be in this field to have a paranormal experience. It might be tied to having a prior experience or just wanting to have that "thrill" associated with it. Many of these types of thrill seekers will not last in this field as most groups will not tolerate this behavior. Most groups who act this way are not around long once members are arrested or lose interest. Most individuals will have at least one paranormal experience in their lives. For most of those people the experiences are not always exciting or thrilling.

Exploring your sensitive or psychic side. Many people have had events happen to them that they consider psychic. Knowing who is on the other end of the phone when it is ringing could be psychic, but if your Mother normally calls you on Monday evenings it may not be so psychic when the phone rings on Monday and you "have a feeling" it is your Mom. Typically, psychic events are not a one time deal. Most psychics will have daily events that lead them to believe they have something "different" about them, though they may not realize it is not normal until talking to others about it. Most psychics or sensitives get enough of a mental workout that they don't need to be involved in a paranormal group. The first thing you need to figure out is if what your experiences are were really psychic to begin with.

When an individual is out to find "proof" of the paranormal they may have one or more avenues in mind. First, may be the personal proof. This is merely proving to themselves that ghosts exist. This might be because of a previous encounter or because of searching for their own spirituality has lead them to trying to prove life exists after death. Many times individuals get caught up in finding their own personal proof and it provides itself as a major distraction to the function of a group. Take for example someone who feels that they have to take a hundred pictures at every hunt or investigation in hopes of finding an orb shot or apparition or records EVPs (electronic voice phenomena; see terminology chapter in resources section) everywhere all the time. They have gone beyond the experience itself and are now focused on the "proof" they hope to find to show to others, so they can prove to themselves that these things truly exist.

Many times groups as a whole will play one part, but will act this way with every piece of evidence they find. They claim to be "scientific" while what they are really trying to do is prove to everyone that they have found their own personal proof. This is when fantasy takes over reality and the group is lost as a whole in this make believe cat and mouse game of the search for answers. This is the big difference between personal and public proof.

Many individuals are in search of public proof, or scientific proof. This has long been the biggest debate with ghost hunters and paranormal investigators. What exactly constitutes "scientific proof" and how can anyone truly provide this? The real answer is we will probably never see this in our lifetimes. An amateur group will find a lot of evidence, but tying any of these pieces together to form a complete picture is very doubtful. There are many other questions that must be answered before anyone can say without a shadow of doubt that ghosts truly exist. Take for example that some type of human consciousness must exist in the dead for it to be able to communicate with the living. It has still yet to be defined and proven to exist in the living. We are still not sure if ghosts exist on their own or if they are a mere perception of the living. This book will not entertain all of the theories, but realize that just because there are hundreds of groups investigating ghosts does not mean they have been proven to exist.

Get rich quick! If you are getting into this field you may have noticed the number of television shows, radio shows, ghost hunting and investigating books, newspaper articles and public tours hosted by ghost groups or individuals. This field has always had its share of people who wanted to be more popular than their neighbor for whatever reason, but in recent years it has become more of who can be more famous.

It seems everyone has written a book or two (yes, this is my first one as well). The popular ghost hunter television shows have driven groups to creating their own public access television shows and personal DVDs to sell from their websites. Groups have been selling t-shirts, tours and certifications on their sites for years, but to be rich or making a living from being a ghost hunter or paranormal investigator? Doubtful.

Many people want to become a professional Parapsychologist and make money from doing this. Most Parapsychologists have another job that puts money on the table for them to pursue this field, ask them. Getting a doctorate in this field could cost you six digits easily and will not pay as glamorous as you might imagine.

Equipment alone is expensive. A decent laptop ($500 +), EMF meters (a good one will fetch $120+), analog and digital recorders ($50+, can run up to $150-$200), cameras ($150+), camcorders ($200+ for night vision, not to mention infrared and other filters), flashlights (cheap, but you will go through many over the years), batteries (a huge expense), more exotic equipment will come with exotic prices. On top of that you'll have to buy something to carry all of this expensive stuff in!

Then you will have to spend money on books and other forms of education, though I have been fortunate to have found many of my books at a half price book store, I have still spent about $1000 on books on various subjects relating to investigating as well as Scientific Journals over the years. There are so many other costs that come with this field (gas for traveling, operating a web site, advertising, etc.) that you will see that will quickly add up. Though some things are cheaper now to be a ghost hunter than it was years ago, imagine not having a digital camera and having to have every picture developed! Bottom line, the expenses are very high and there is no way to really skimp by in this field.

This leads me to my next question that you must ask yourself. What are you willing to commit to this field? This goes beyond money and begs for what amount of time you will be able to give to a group as well as your own education and research. A decent group can desire a couple of days during the week for meetings about the group or about investigations and interviews. Then there is the time online since most groups are internet driven to some extent (e-mails, message boards and chat sessions) as well as your own research time (reading, online, etc.).

I try to balance a full-time job and a marriage as well as a life in-between pursuing other interests (obviously to a time-suffered lesser degree) while working this field as a full-time effort beyond a mere hobby. We have general meetings to get the group together at minimum once a month (typically twice), meetings prior to investigations as well as after the investigations. Of course then there is going to the investigations themselves as well as interviews prior to the investigations. Also, can't forget interviews of potential members. To be successful at this field you are looking at having to be involved with the field daily, if not for just a few hours a day. It doesn't sound all that bad, but believe me, the time adds up quick. You will find yourself wanting and needing more and more time as you get deeper into this field and your demands begin to press. It can drain you as well as your loved ones around you.

Chapter 4: The Reality

You've seen the television shows and web sites and can not wait to jump in! Hopefully, you realize that what you see on television isn't completely real, but what are you in for?

In being a paranormal investigator, dealing with the public is your greatest obstacle. Interviewing potential investigators if you wish to start your own group can be trying at times. Interviewing clients can be a completely different ordeal.

In my and other's investigations I have been a part of, I have seen and dealt with clients who suffered from drug and alcohol abuse. I have heard reports of spousal abuse and groups have seen signs of child abuse. These are very difficult things to deal with, especially if you are not prepared for them. They may be the cause of the paranormal events (or an additional factor to them) or the "events" may be a cry for attention or help. They are also very difficult things to talk with the client about and create other dilemmas that extend beyond being an investigator of the paranormal.

There are the occasional unintentional fraud cases. Ones that the homeowner was certain a ghost was responsible for certain activity, but it might just be their pets, rodents (squirrels, termites, raccoons, etc.) or another logical event that will make everyone involved very embarrassed that they felt it was once considered paranormal. This is why it is so important to search every possible logical answer first!

You will also occasionally stumble across those that will attempt to deceive you intentionally. Some people want to see if they can fool a ghost hunting group or some merely just want to see how they work or have them visit so they will create a story just for you.

Most people are honest about what is happening to them and are not crazy or have addictions, but the events that happen to them can intimidate even the most seasoned paranormal investigator.

Some investigations deal with apparitions that are actually assaulting the people in the house. Though very rare, you may encounter cases of families that are being scratched or otherwise physically harmed. Other cases may deal with events that affect children physically or emotionally. These are the toughest cases to investigate and have forced more than one person I have worked with to leave the field.

We must realize we can greatly affect the outcome of someone's life by the opinions and knowledge we share. The ideas we share may make someone want to move out of their house and experience financial burden or cause tension or stress which can affect many aspects of their lives. We come into contact with children who are experiencing these things that not even their parents are able to deal with. Their parents will look to you to help their children through these times. Are you ready for this responsibility?

There is also another reality behind what we do. That is, the reality that ghosts do not actually exist. According to science, ghosts do not exist and are not real. Though dozens of parapsychologists have documented and investigated thousands of cases over the last Century, none of them have ever been proven to be verifiable completely.

Ghostly events are typically spontaneous (therefore experiments are doomed to fail) and can not be created, captured or asked to act on cue to be documented by various sources on a repeated basis. It's been very frustrating to study over the past one hundred and twenty plus years. It has lead many to believe that the chase is fruitless and will never provide anything outside of hopeful or misleading evidence.

    I say all of these negative sounding things not to sway you from getting involved in this field, but to prepare you. Most people have no idea what they are getting into when they decide to join or start a group. The fancy web sites you see do not explain the details behind their "professional" pursuits and television does little to demonstrate what you truly go through on a day to day basis.

Part II: Getting Started

Chapter 1: Education

You have already taken one of the greatest steps one can take as a potential paranormal investigator or ghost hunter. You are reading this book. Reading books is probably the most important thing you can do to help you gain knowledge of this field, no matter what level you consider yourself or where you wish to end up.

Field experience is fine, but if you have no idea what has been researched or previously theorized about what you are doing your experiences are severely limited. Without the advice and insight of those who have come before you, the things you experience in the field will not be fully understood or may not be relevant enough to help those who look to you for insight into what is happening.

I'm not saying the book you are reading here will be the sum of your knowledge, but quite the contrary. I encourage you to read other books that teach you how to become more knowledgeable in this field. I would encourage you to read as much as you can from as many different viewpoints as possible, including the skeptical views as well.

I have included a list of books in Part IV of this book that have helped me over the years. It is not a complete list of books on this subject, but only ones that I can vouch for that provides helpful meanings toward a healthy pursuit of information.

I have also taken the time to split these books into various categories that can help you focus on the type of learning or information you desire. Some individuals get caught up in certain types of books, but the best thing to do is to sample a variety of books and from different authors.

Many people get hung up on the "ghost story" type of book. While there is nothing wrong with this style of book, it limits what the reader will truly learn about this field. There are a handful of books out there that take a story and treat it more like an investigation or add more behind the story to make it worthwhile for the reader.

Many Parapsychology books read like text books (since many of them are or were). These should not be viewed as books that border on the fringe of ghost hunting like many groups treat them. Many of the books listed under Parapsychology will give you more education about ghosts that many amateur ghost hunters know from years in the field.

Also, be willing to reach out into other fields of science and general knowledge that can add to your understanding that will greatly assist you in the field and help separate loose theories from actual knowledge (physics, meteorology, geology, psychology, counseling, forensics, home construction, electronics, plumbing, magic, even pest management and so on.). You will be amazed (and sometimes flustered) at the different types of knowledge that you will have to dig in to while investigating claims of the paranormal. Lastly, if you are using tools in the field be sure to read about their actual use before taking the advice of what is written on the internet about their usage in ghost hunting situations as the tools used in this field were not designed to find ghosts.

You have obviously already started looking at paranormal websites as an information source. While this is good there are a few things you should be warned about. Many of these groups on the internet do not have the experience they are touting. Many of their theories or findings are cut and pasted from other sites or other people's ideas and are loosely translated. Many sites are merely fronts for people who are not involved directly with the field, but wish they could be. Granted, while these types of sites are few they can affect the newbie in how they view this field and the basic beliefs that they will hold.

The next best thing to reviewing sites and reading books will be interacting with others who share your interest. The internet is a great place to start as you can roam around and test various message boards to share your views as well as view those of others. Message boards have become a pain over the years due to the lack of "family atmosphere". You used to be able to sign up under a company's service and view dozens of various message boards (I.e., ezboard, board host), but now it seems that every web site has its own customized service. This means you may have to sign up for every message board you plan to visit. It also means you will not be as likely to be a consistent contributor (as will others). Message boards are not as flourishing with information as they once were, but they are still a source of knowledge and interaction. They can also be useful to meet others in your area that shares your interests and pursuits.

This leads to the next step; working with a group. If you plan on working with a group or starting your very own the first step should always be working with another local group. If you have decided to form your own group already it would still be in your best interest to work with local groups to help you refine your techniques as well as learn things from others in the field.

It is a lot harder to work cases than you can imagine. Gaining practical experience alongside a "seasoned" individual is an intelligent move that will help you in the future no matter what your long term goals are. Even if your intentions are to work as a weekend ghost hunter or hobbyist, a knowledgeable person by your side will be indispensable to the growth of knowledge through experience.

When you have decided what it is you are searching for be sure to look for a group that seems to share your same goals. Do not look at what you are getting into as a commitment at this point; you should just be out for the experience of being in a group. Be sure to ask them plenty of questions so that your time with them is productive for the both of you and not end up as a negative experience.

What are their goals? Experiences? How long have any of them been involved with paranormal investigation or ghost hunting? Have they read any books that you have? Have they read anything at all with this subject? How often do they work cases? When do they typically meet up? How will this work with your schedule? How do they go about investigating cases? Do they require a fee to join? Do they work with other groups or belong as a spin-off or charter of another group? What type of training do they offer?

Be wary of them if they don't ask you questions that pertain to your background and knowledge. Don't be afraid to be truthful about your knowledge and experiences. If you have read a handful of books you may find yourself more educated than most.

Also, be wary of groups that charge for you to participate with group activities. They should be providing you with something more than just tagging along for you to have to pay to work along side of them. Many groups collect dues (and charge clients) to help pay for their expenses, but what are they really providing for that money and is it worth it to you?

The latest trend in paranormal groups is to offer training courses and certificates. Where is their knowledge coming from and is a certificate from their particular organization really going to get you anything other than a bill? Be cautious if a group you are potentially looking to work with offers this to you, though if it sounds (and is priced) reasonable then it might not hurt to listen to what someone else has to say. But always remember, most of what is out there as far as knowledge is really circulated opinions and loose theories.

When working with a group always be sure to let your intentions be known up front. It could be the difference between a working relationship between two groups and an all-out paranormal group bash-fest. Be honest and upfront with the owner of the group as to what you would like to do in the future and hopefully they will help you toward attaining your goal, or at least not be surprised when you leave to form your own group.

Chapter 2: Starting Your Own Group

So, you've decided you want to start your own group. There are pros and cons to both, as you have probably witnessed if you worked with other groups. This is not a decision that should be taken half-heartedly as you have to understand that once you start this many people will rely on your decisions.

The biggest pro for starting your own group is that, well, it's your group. You can run it by yourself or have your sister or best friend help you. Many groups have "Founders" and "Co-founders". This helps split up the responsibilities without having to rely on your investigators to take control of your group. This also helps alleviate some of the potential financial burdens that may arise to operating a group.

In running your own group you have your own freedom to approach this field however you want. You will not be confined to someone else's opinions or direction. Just be sure yours is clearer than you neighbors.

You will have the opportunity to build your own team from the types of people you want to bring together (more on this in chapter three).

Of course, there are downsides to operating your own group. It is your group. Anything that goes wrong because of the group is your responsibility. You are responsible for its financial support, advertising, growth and nurturing as well as organizing, planning and execution for all events and cases (unless you delegate!). No matter how involved you plan on getting, it is still a potentially large personal and financial investment.

If you share ownership with someone else, be sure to have plans for what will happen to the group if one of you decides to depart unexpectedly. Many groups have been disbanded quickly when one of the leaders has decided to move on abruptly.

In operating a group you will be in competition with a number of groups that will certainly already occupy your area. Some groups don't take too kindly on those who move into "their territory" and some will let you know this. Along the same lines you also must understand that you will be competing for private cases and will either benefit or suffer from the public's experience with this group (or others) if you are attempting to do hunts on private property.

In starting your own group it would be wise to start the group before forming a web site. Many groups do this the other way around. To me it's putting the cart before the horse. Granted, a web site can help bring attention to the fact that there is a group and it needs some members. Your city may also have a public message board on its local Government page or in an online newspaper site that can help you advertise for help.

There are other avenues to look at on the internet. Meetup.com is a service that offers a place for individuals to gather as groups that have a similar interest. There are many paranormal groups that have started on this service or exist within this service as clubs that get together. Many of these clubs are merely social clubs, which give those interested a chance to discuss with others their interest in this field without being depended upon as a piece of a group.

You may try posting advertisements in public libraries or local colleges for members, just be sure to get permission first. Many groups are formed around friends, colleagues or acquaintances who share an interest in discovering this field. Don't be afraid to ask people you already know. You would be surprised to find out who has an interest in this field or potential paranormal experiences for that matter.

The next biggest task is creating a web site to advertise your group to the public, other groups and other potential members whom you may need to expand your current lineup or fill due to attrition.

The easiest bet is to utilize a free web site host on the internet. My first web site was a free site hosted by Geocities.com, in 2000 I moved to Angelfire where my old site still exists to this day. In 2007, I decided to obtain my own domain (GhostHelp.net) which is hosted by Bravenet.com.

The big problem with free sites is that your web site name will be very boring and will not sound "professional" and your site will have a lot of advertising tied to it. Geocities, Angelfire, tripod, 50megs, bravenet and a list of others can host your site for free. These sites also offer extra storage and bandwidth (more visitors as well as more sophisticated things you can afford to run on your site) for various prices per month. They all also offer hosting options if you desire to secure your own domain (which they can all help you do) and you will be able to pay through them to secure your site on their computers for a predetermined amount of time.

The biggest difference between these companies is what they will offer you to tie in with your sites as well as their ease of use. The more they offer, or the easier they are to use, the more they will cost you if you decide to upgrade. If you have little or no knowledge of html then I would suggest a company that it is easy to design using their software. If you desire to design your own site using personal software then they are all about the same.

I have designed sites using the above companies and I have found Bravenet to be the easiest to use. I like to write my own code and their setup with files and viewing has been much easier for me to use than my old site on Angelfire. Of course, this is just a matter of opinion and I did use Angelfire for over seven years! It depends completely on your skills with html or web design and how often you plan on updating your site.

Most paranormal web sites are about the same. They all have a message board, information about what kinds of cases they are doing, an "about us" page and a links page. The key is to do something on your site or with your group that you share on your site to stick out amongst the weeds.

Most groups are taking this to the attention-getting aspect of creating their own pod casts or radio shows, you-tube videos or selling their own classes or tours from their sites. If you plan on doing this be sure your host will allow this if it is free. Also, be sure that it doesn't appear that you're merely in this to make a buck (hopefully you aren't one of those!).

Once your group is set up and you have your online world set up it's time to get out there and investigate, or at least have meetings. I suggest having meetings at least once a month to meet and discuss topics about the group as well as past, present or future cases or investigations. It gives the group more time to work and communicate together which will be extremely important when you get into the field.

The setting doesn't matter as long as it is convenient for all of your members who will be attending. I try to find a central public location to have a meeting. A place that eventually closes gives the meetings a definitive time scale and won't drag itself out until the wee hours of the morning. Of course, it always helps to be organized for these meetings in advance by having notes typed up for what you will cover.

These meetings will also give you the opportunity to see how involved members are willing to be. If they don't seem too upset to continuously miss meetings do not be afraid to end their relationship with the group. Your members will appreciate that you care about the survivability of the group and will make them realize you are serious about running the group (and will keep them from missing meetings!).

I would also suggest having meetings (or internet chat sessions) prior to heading out to an investigation or case. This gives everyone ample time to become familiar with the information you need to share with them prior to the case so that your time will be spent more efficiently on site. It also gives an opportunity to carpool to the location.

After an investigation or hunt it is also important to have a meeting within a day or so of the event. This keeps the information fresh in your mind and will give you the chance to share insight and early information about what you have just experienced. After a few more days you will want to get together again to review you information and data together (probably in a little more private setting).

With starting a group you will have a plethora of decisions to make. Many of these you can decide for yourself in advance (or with your Co-founder). Some will come up for debate when you have formed your group. One of the biggest topics is to charge or not charge for investigations. This has been a hot topic for a number of years and has valid arguments for both sides.

Investigations are not cheap. There is a lot of equipment utilized and typically a degree of traveling to the site numerous times (typically three times; before, during and after) as well as time is spent pursuing an individual case. Many groups merely ask for their travel to be paid for while others may impose a flat fee in addition to charging travel or mileage.

Personally, I don't find the practice responsible or ethical. We are amateurs who are doing this mostly for our own entertainment or research while attempting to help the homeowner. When we attempt to help a homeowner we are providing a slight service, but no one can guarantee results. If an individual wishes to reimburse us at their own request I will initially turn down the request, but for some individuals paying for your time or service gives them a sense of accomplishment or closure about what is happening.

On the flip side, if you desire to conduct a hunt on private property you may find yourself having to pay for that privilege. In many cases it is worth it, but the best advice is to dig deep into the history of the area first. Don't rely on the internet to give you what you are looking for as these may just be urban legends or stories. Dig into the history of a location to see if any of the stories may be true before wasting your time investigating them.

Another topic is that of getting your group into a newspaper or on television. I will discuss this in more detail in chapter four. Before you can get your group on T.V. you're going to have to find the right kind of people first.

Chapter 3: Getting Investigators

Always interview a potential member in person before deciding to include them in the group. A person can seem like Fox Mulder online, but until you meet them face to face and discuss matters in person you can never be sure what they are really like. Be very up front and black and white to them of what you are looking for as far as investigators. Be sure they are not too controlling or overly opinionated. These traits will drive others away from your group and will be disruptive to the growth and advancement of the group.

Don't be afraid to be selective. Believe me, there are hundreds of people just like you who want to get into investigating and ghost hunting. There are hundreds more already in groups that may soon dissipate and will need a new place to carry on their quest. Being honest with someone who will not be a good fit in the group will be one of the most important things you will do for the future and growth of your group. You're in charge so don't be afraid to take charge!

If possible, invite them to a meeting as their initial interview. Again, be clear to them that this is merely a meeting to see if you (or the group) wishes to acquire their services. If you desire to have an open group that accepts everyone as members you will have to give them less control over what the group does or face having internal problems that can rip it apart. Specifying members as well as their roles is the safest bet to keep your group around for the long haul.

Always look to add someone that will not only mesh with your current thoughts about the subject but will also bring varying ideas to the table. Hopefully, you will also be able to bring in people of varying experience in investigating as well. A blend of experience and inexperience always keeps the feel of the group fresh and the inexperienced ones will challenge those with experience through asking questions and looking for instruction.

Another aspect that will strengthen the group will be bringing in people who excel in certain areas that of need to be successful in this field. Someone with a background in counseling or photography can be a great asset to the group. Typically, everyone is good at something or has a particular strength in a field that might yield an unforeseen strength for the group down the road. Who knows, the guy you brought in who is an animal expert might be able to identify signs of animals that could be causing events in a home.

Here is an abbreviated list of what I ask potential investigators before I officially give them the nod:

1. Have you worked with another paranormal group in the past (or currently)? If so, find out how long and why they left. If they are still currently with them then why are they branching out to other groups?

2. What makes this group your choice over the multitude of other groups in this area? Is it your fancy website or your ideals that seemed to have brought this person to you?

3. What are your specific goals with investigating the paranormal (other than personal experience or finding "proof")? Find out if they have a specific goal in mind. Are they just going to do this for a little while or are they willing to stay for the long haul?

4. On what do you base your knowledge of how paranormal groups operate? (Be specific of book, television program, web sites or other type of media.). This will give you an idea as to how they feel about the paranormal or what opinions they may have about it. This question may also bring about a personal event that has happened to them in the past. They may have dug into the paranormal because of this. If they wish to solve personal questions or relieve personal demons they may not be around as long as someone who is in search of finding outward answers or helping the public.

5. What other aspects of your personality or other things about you can help us? Are they really outgoing? Maybe they can help set up hunts or investigations. Do they love to research? Are they a night owl? This general question will give you their personal answer as to what they feel is their biggest personal strength that can help in investigations. It is here that you will hear if they feel they are psychic or not (if you haven't heard already).

6. Do you possess an education or technical background that can assist us in investigating? (Photography, scientist, web designer, counselor, etc.)

7. How long of a notice would you need if you were needed to assist in a potential case (or other group activity)? Find out what they are able to commit to you and the group. This is critical to the survivability of your group. If they work full time and are a full time student they will have little time to help you. It seems that everyone is available for meetings, but when a case hits everyone will suddenly be busy. Be sure to know what is going on in their lives so you can better plan out things in advance. Of course you will always want to set things up after confirming members can attend.

8. Are there specific days and or times that you are available to meet with the group for meetings? Use this information to plan weekly or monthly meetings. Find a common day and time that everyone can agree to meet. People will fight you on this but you have to make the majority rule. This may eventually alienate people from the group; you will never be able to prevent this from happening once in a while. The key is to make it work for a majority or the most involved of the group.

9. (If mother/daughter or husband/wife) would one or the other be available to investigate if the other is not or is this a package deal? Transportation and reliability. If a husband/wife, Mother /Daughter or Father/Son or roommates/best friends wish to join, will they both not go if one is unable to attend a meeting or investigation? Is this worth the gamble?

Basically, what are they looking for in this field? Why are they looking at your group and not looking at someone else's? What are their true motives? What can they bring to the table to help the group operate and grow? Will they be available when you need them?

If they say they have had personal experiences that they felt were paranormal be sure to ask them to be specific about event and how it made them feel. Is exploring this feeling why they want to join? Those in search of these answers do not stay around long typically. Investigating for personal reasons never seem to last as long as those who are in search of the big picture or helping others.

Others may claim to have "abilities" or claim to be psychic or sensitive. Many of these individuals mean well, but they may be misinterpreting one or more events as more than coincidence. Just be mindful that there are those who are sensitive and it's just trying to figure out if bringing them in will be an asset or a distraction.

A psychic or sensitive can be helpful in investigations and hunts as they can use their "tool" to help, but what is their motivation for wanting to display their abilities? If their ego may outweigh their usefulness then it might be in your best interest to avoid them. Some psychics may have strange practices or beliefs that may conflict with investigators or homeowners of cases or might just be a downright distraction.

Be wary if the psychic or sensitive is focused on their "feeling" or on always being right. These types of psychics are typically only looking to impress everyone and may even argue "facts" of what is or has happened at the sight. A true psychic knows they will not be right most of the time and will ask more questions than attempt to state facts. You should be aware that cold reading is done in a similar fashion by giving random general clues based upon clues of those around them.

Basically, you should view those who claim to possess these abilities like all other investigators you look to bring aboard. Will they be a good fit for the team and not cause conflict or confusion? Will they work well with the clients? Will they be able to bring something of use to the group? Remember that they will have their own ideas about ghosts or may know nothing at all about what you know. Be sure that they will be a good fit no matter what their "powers" may indicate.

As a group you must decide what to do and where to go. Not just for investigations or hunts, but what the future brings. You may have your own idea, but you must embrace the dreams of your investigators as well. If you want to keep the group small and out of the public eye and they all want to have dozens of members and get the groups name in lights you may be forced to find a happy medium.

Chapter 4: Getting Noticed

Once establishing your group and a place to meet and a website to be seen, you'll find the desire to be like other groups and get noticed in the public eye. Many groups rush out and try to get into their local paper hoping that this will make them celebrities. Other groups attempt to get on television via local access or by merely creating their own videos for you-tube.

Until you have established yourself after a few

private investigations or numerous ghost hunts there should be no real reason to brag what you have done or who you are. A properly written website will be enough to bring you cases on a consistent basis and there are always locations to be hunted. Patience will bring you the opportunities you will need to be seen based upon what you have done in this field. Public exposure is a tricky thing and if you get too greedy it can certainly make things a mess for you and your group.

Many groups do not think about the repercussions of putting their name to print so early in their careers. If there is one thing you must learn about the press is that if you want to expose yourself for what you do the press will definitely expose you for what you do. You might think your group is the cat's meow, but anything you say will be fair game to be printed and interpreted by the reporter. If you try to make it about your group the article will definitely look self-centered. If you make it about the field itself with a little advertising sprinkled in you should look pretty good to most of the public.

The press in general does not have a positive view on ghost hunters. Granted, there is the occasional upbeat and positive story about a group that is nothing more than an advertisement. This is the type you want, but good luck convincing the writer to make you look good.

The more you put your group out in the public beyond the part that is looking for you the more you risk attack from those who disagree with what you do. A majority of the public does not understand us and what we do and there are a lot of individuals and groups that are skeptical in nature that will have a field day with you if they are to read your article. Basically, be ready for all types of feedback (or none at all) if you wish to put your group out there.

As far as putting videos on the internet I'm not a big fan. First, you are telling potential clients that you are willing to put information out in the public eye (more on this in the next chapter). Second, many sites that feature personal videos are full of fakes and frauds when it comes to the paranormal and other subjects related to it. Typically groups try to feature their "proof" or "evidence", but who is really taking any of this seriously?

One of the best ways of getting noticed typically occurs during what I call the "silly season" or what the normal people call October 31, Halloween. There are many social groups, companies or other organizations that like to have a speaker present information to them periodically. When the calendar flips to October, the interest in paranormal groups shifts into high gear.

Public speaking is far more effective in advertising your group than a newspaper article. With your speech you alone will be influencing the crowd and not relying on someone else to put your thoughts together. Listening to a good public speaker can be very motivating, influential and persuasive when it comes to the content at hand.

Speaking in public helps you personally in a variety of ways. Public speaking gives the public a sense that you are a leader, it will give your group notice to the public that it knows what it's talking about. It will also make you a better communicator overall and will definitely boost your confidence in yourself and the subject.

Public speaking helps you for this field in that you have to study for it and recite it as well as answer questions. It will expand your knowledge and put more questions on the table as well as give you many examples of what is happening out there. I'll bet that nearly everyone there will have an experience to share. One of the greatest learning experiences comes when you have to teach what you know. You'll experience this first when you begin to interview for positions within the group.

Most organizations will book lectures months in advance, so if you are looking to contact an organization, do it as early as possible. When booking a lecture or speech be sure to get specifics about the size of the group as well as what their interest is in the field. Also, find out the time frame in which you have to speak so your speech can be planned out ahead of time as well as what you will have at your disposal at the location (power source to display laptop, a table to set up your tools and business cards, a P.A. system if it is a larger room, food or refreshments, etc.).

Be sure to bring plenty of business cards and brochures and any other handouts you feel are pertinent to what you are speaking about.

Chapter 5: Common Pitfalls

The average group starts out small and investigates local areas that are purportedly haunted. They may hunt in cemeteries or old abandoned buildings and eventually get their feet wet investigating a first-person account of a current apparitional event or haunting in a private residence. Then, after six months to a year the group is gone.

What happened? Why does the average group last less than two years in this field and why is this field not advancing? These are a couple of very valid questions. The reality is that both of these questions are intertwined and that one is responsible for the other.

There are multiple reasons for groups to fail or to slowly disappear into the "404- file not found" sector of the internet and reality. We'll look at a few of the most popular ones that I feel affect groups today or that I know personally have caused the demise of a former group. Hopefully, this will help you avoid the similar fate of teams that have hung up their acronyms for good.

- **Having vague goals when starting out.** Some groups merely want to experience a ghost. This is fine, but do you have to form a ghost hunting team to do this? For some it is finding "proof" of ghosts. Well, how are your planning to do this? You must define what you want from this experience and build a path to accomplish it. The biggest problem with most individuals as well as teams is that they fail to really accomplish anything in this field once they learn the basics and have a few experiences. This leads to losing interest and leads to the person or group leaving the field.
- **Rushing into investigations or hunts.** This problem can be threefold. First, you may not be prepared for what you are experiencing (or what you think you are experiencing) and may interpret your experiences incorrectly if you have not done your homework prior. Second, if you rush into an investigation you are setting yourself and the client up for failure. How can you expect to help someone through a situation when you are not knowledgeable in what they are

experiencing? Third, you might not be prepared for the long haul that is in front of you. If you have not taken the time to realize how much work and how many hours you will have to dedicate to this field you will most certainly fail. Ghost hunting can be a weekend event, but eventually it will consume more and more time, if you are not prepared for this you will eventually have to make choices.

- **Many groups are not willing to come up with new ideas or direction for their group or challenge old ideas that are believed as fact.** Experimentation in various areas of this field as well as pursuing your own personal theories can help a group stay healthy and avoid becoming stagnant. Getting involved in new areas or shifting the groups overall focus can also spark life into a group before everyone gets bored. Along with this goes falling for the belief systems in place blindly without knowing the why and how they are in place. Many websites are full of theories that are stated as facts. If you are not willing to challenge old ideas by doing your own work your group will eventually become boring to those within it. Many groups are not willing to adapt to new ideas and concepts brought into the field unless they personally come up with them. This is plain ignorance. It is fine to disagree or challenge these theories, but do the work to prove or disprove.

Part of the scientific method is that someone else must follow up on what someone else has previously done to either confirm or question the results. This is called self-correcting behavior and is the cornerstone in creating scientific facts.

- **Releasing private information to the public.** This one can be a quick career ender and can also lead to legal issues. When dealing with the public you have to know when to keep information private. Blabbing about a case on a message board or showing a case on you-tube without the homeowner's permission can lead to some serious trouble for you as well as the entire field. Be sure to use confidentiality forms when investigating a private residence. Be careful what you say in public or post on the internet about anyone, especially when it comes to your cases and when you are talking about murders or any other public information in dealing with individuals.

- **Trespassing.** This one can also lead to legal issues or worse. Part of researching a site is finding out who to contact to get permission to enter. It becomes increasingly harder to gain access to sites when people take the cheating route.

- **Not communicating with other groups.** This is not only a pitfall; it is a big pet peeve amongst established groups. When a new group pops up all you receive is an e-mail asking to exchange links, that's it. There is so much you can learn if you just ask someone else for a little help. Every new group wants to make their own path without the help of anyone else. The problem is they are walking in the same footsteps and reading the same writing on the wall. The established groups can save you a lot of trouble with your learning curve (as I am trying to do here) if newbies just tried to communicate. This ill-communication tends to lead to groups becoming territorial or just plain act like they are in high school. The investigators and clients are the ones hurt in this immature act as well as the loss of information that a group has gained when it shuts down without passing it on.

- **Want/need/desire for fame and media attention**. I'm not sure when this became trendy, but I'd say television had a lot to do with it. Some groups put their name in a newspaper to help get cases; others do it to make themselves look good (usually that's not possible). Putting your group in a newspaper with the intention of getting your name out there for publicity toward the general public isn't a bad thing. This can help you get cases and make you appear as your article paints your group. The problem stems from when groups do it just to get their name in the newspaper, there is a difference. Groups are putting themselves on radio as well as television (typically local access) at astounding rates, but do they really provide the public with anything useful? Are they being ethical? Are they really educated about this field enough to be teaching others about it?

- **Putting themselves at the top of the hierarchy of groups without merit**. Nothing starts a turf war faster than a group that claims to be better than the rest. Many groups have claims that make them "different" than others, in which they feel makes them better. If they do their homework they might find that they are just like all the other groups, except for the fact that they have an overblown ego. Groups that act this way are not respected by others in this field and give the public a bad taste in their mouth when they have to see ghost hunting politics on websites. If someone reads that you are so much better than other groups they'll wonder why you have to make such a statement and might actually go find these other groups to see what they are really about. This type of attitude usually wins no friends and your future in this field will be limited to your ability to change your attitude.

- **Becoming part of a "family" or parent organization**. Many groups do this when they first start out since they feel this may be a ticket to the big time, or they may just feel this will help them advance in the field. Parent organizations sometimes feed other groups cases and "teach" them their thoughts and theories. Either way, you are truly nothing more than a puppet for the lead organization. This limits your beliefs (that is, if the parent org actually communicates with you) and puts you in the hands of someone else. If they, or another group in the organization, does something illegal or brings negative press against them it could tear the entire organization apart instantly leaving groups to actually fend for themselves. Don't get me wrong, working together is good, but a group working for another group is pointless and potentially dangerous. Larger "families" instill beliefs and theories that may not have any reality behind them and may be conjured to keep the interest in their favor. Groups should form their own beliefs and create their own theories from their own work. If someone provides you with a theory of their own be sure they demonstrate the work behind that theory so that you may go out in the field and test it yourself. That's real science.

- **Groups that focus on creating an "empire"**. Some groups want to be so well known that they create their own World that revolves around them. Based on general beliefs about this field they may create a message board or other type of public forum of communication which is dedicated to the self. These types may also be out for money based upon this field, which may provide them profit from the field but the field will never profit from them. Other self-serving groups may just be so involved with their socializing about what they do that they eventually do nothing but socialize. Many groups get so wrapped up in message boards or public meetings that they end up making a "career" in one or the other and ultimately never work in the field again. These "hiatus status" people eventually work their way out of this field over time.

Part III: Getting Involved - Conducting an Investigation or Hunt

Chapter 1 Initial Contact

This is the moment you have waited for. Hopefully you didn't skip to this part of the book! As a paranormal investigator, and especially as a group owner, you will be approached by the public via e-mail, telephone or in public depending on how you advertise your group.

The most traditional way is by way of your website through e-mail or a form sender. Typically, people who are e-mailing you about their problem are reaching out to you for help and they will normally be nervous or intimidated to do so. The key here is to make the point of contact easy to find, easy to use and make the person feel comfortable about contacting you. A website with intense graphics of skulls and the theme to "Ghostbusters" may seem cute to you, but remember your audience when designing your site and contact methods.

Using a form gives you extra options that basic e-mail can not. With e-mail you can only fill in the subject line, which can help you to find out a particular page where they are e-mailing you from if you have contact points on various pages. A form gives you the opportunity to ask for information up front (name, city, state, reason for contact, etc.). I suggest keeping it simple since people will contact you for various reasons.

When an e-mail comes in about a person needing help it will typically be somewhat vague. They will probably explain things in a nutshell as well as the latest developments. The first thing you should do whenever you receive any e-mail pertaining to your group is to respond immediately. This says a lot about a group and about what type of organization it is.

When responding to the e-mail, do not be judgmental. You may feel the need to judge their experience because what you are reading sounds improbable or textbook, but do not disagree or agree with what is happening. The person will be happy that someone is responding to them and will feel less "crazy" that they may have felt before they contacted someone. Giving in to unfounded fears and experiences or saying something isn't possible at this point will not benefit the other person or your standing with them.

Preparing the response you will want to give the initial e-mail a basic analysis. What are they looking for? Help? Someone to solve their problem or just someone to report this to? If they seemingly need help you can ask if they request an onsite investigation or merely an interview with a couple of investigators (don't be pushy).

You will want more detail about what is happening and in a second e-mail they will usually let you have it. Ask when the events started and have them give it to you from beginning to current as best as possible. This will help you see if events are increasing in frequency or intensity, which can help you determine if an investigation is necessary. Another good tip is to have them begin to document the events and as much detail about them as possible, this will help them remember specifics about individual events at a later date.

Another important aspect of the follow-up e-mail is to provide them with comfort, help ease their fears and let them know they are not "crazy" since there are other people out there who are experiencing what they are experiencing. The situation is created from their connection to whatever is occupying their house with them; since they are living they have the upper hand in the situation. The person may not feel like it, but remind them that they are truly in control of the situation no matter how out-of-hand it may seem. In these situations it is typically just a matter of confidence that changes how things are happening in the home or location.

When corresponding with the individual do not make it seem like they will need or rely on you to get through this situation. It's understandable that you want to investigate this place, but you must always keep the homeowner's health and well being before your personal desires. Some individuals will not like this approach and will move on to another group (believe me; many people contact more than one group). Most importantly, they must remain in control of their situation since they are the ones with the connection to the ghost (or other problem) and ultimately they are the one that must work through it.

If the person wishes for you to contact them via telephone be sure this case is one worth going after. Once the person has your number you may receive phone calls at all hours no matter what your request. If you decide to call the person, be sure to have the facts provided from them as well as a list of questions in front of you. Many times I will send them an e-mail to gather some more information. Based on their response I will set up a phone interview if this is their wish. You can also attempt to schedule an interview in person at the residence or in another public location if they desire.

The telephone interview is obviously much easier to gather information from, but with a follow-up there will be a lot to write down as well as digest as you are helping the person. People generally feel that with their initial vague e-mail you will have an answer for them, be prepared to field that question. Also note that an overwhelming majority of cases with contact, as well as the person experiencing the events, will be from females.

From the response to your initial reply you will have much more data and facts to deal with. The case may seem a bit different than you may have first thought and usually adds information that makes the case a lot more difficult to interpret than what you first thought.

The first thing you will want to do is print the response out or put it into a work processor program. This will help you pull key elements out of the e-mail (or highlight them) for follow-up questions or to help create a timeline. I typically read the e-mail and write notes as I read through it. Developing a timeline helps you understand who is being affected and if the events are getting more intense or are happening with more frequency. If there is an increase in frequency or intensity, as stated earlier, it may indicate that there needs to be some intervention by your group at this point to help the homeowner through the events (you didn't just think you would get an invitation to set up your gear and campout in someone's house, did you?).

After initially responding to the potential client I like to copy and paste their information and case outline in a folder on my computer. Keeping information organized and private is key to being a success in this field. I also have my own filing system that I use to keep track of cases. It may seem neat at first to have case names like "The James Case", but after a while you will forget what happened with each case. I number the cases based upon the order they are received during the month of a particular year. The fifth case of February, 2008, for example, is case number 050208. I use this method since it keeps my cases in order in a folder that I create by year and by month on my computer. When saving 050208 I will also put the persons name and a few key words to keep my memory fresh when I have a dozen or more cases piled up in the February file (ex., 050208 James shadow figures dresser movement).

One last thing on keeping files, be sure to back them up once in a while by storing them somewhere other than your hard drive (like on a CD) so if your computer crashes your group's history won't as well. More than once I've lost data in different ways. It's very heartbreaking to lose any information you have gathered in the field.

Based upon their second response you will want to form questions around the events they describe to either help them find a logical answer or provide your own. Hopefully, you will be able to secure an onsite interview with the client, since it will most certainly allow you to begin a basic walkthrough investigation of the area and will help you come up with possible logical explanations.

If the case seems like one worth pursuing, ask the homeowner if they would like you to come out to investigate either by phone or e-mail. Remember to not be pushy, but to let them know that a visit can be easier to interview and will help you understand what is happening by being there in person. Hopefully, you have established where this person lives prior to asking to come out and investigate (so you're not driving from Ohio to Nebraska).

If you send them an e-mail it will be up to the homeowner as to the course of action to take. Don't ask too many follow-up questions in your e-mail (it will take longer for them to respond and may give them a reason to cease contact with you) and let them know there are plenty of other questions you have. A telephone interview, again, can help expedite the communication process and can take the place of an on site interview, but being in the location allows you to put places and faces to the events.

Chapter 2: Art of Interviewing

This chapter is written with the thought that you are now in the client's house and are ready to begin your interview and investigation. Be sure to find out when the homeowner is available and then check with your investigators before agreeing to a date and time.

Always show up on time and always be prepared for the interview. Have all of your questions typed up in advance as well as all the correspondence between you and the client. Be sure to bring something to write on and with and be sure to not bring what you won't need. If you decide to bring your equipment be sure to not lug all of it in the house in a bunch of big cases if the client is only expecting an interview.

Why interview? We have all the information about the case, why can't we just do an investigation? The interview is the most important part of the investigation, contrary to what you might believe from reading websites or watching paranormal shows on television. The important information rests with the experiences of those who witnessed the events. If you get the most information out of those experiences and are able to find relationships with events and what causes them it may make a physical investigation a evidence gathering success. Without interviewing witnesses you are really fishing in the dark, without bait and without a pole.

Upon entering the home your investigation should begin with a visual examination of the home. In other words, what types of interests do you see displayed on their walls? Do they enjoy skiing or have an interest in the occult? These visual clues can help you in breaking the ice with small talk and can also give you clues to their motives or belief systems. Being aware of your surroundings is critical once you are onsite; always keep your eyes and ears ready for spontaneous events that may occur without warning. With this in mind, always be ready to find logical explanations to explain the individual events they may be experiencing in particular areas.

The environment for the interview should contain as few distractions as possible (children playing in room, guests over to see the ghost hunters, dishwasher running, etc.). Let the homeowner know exactly how you are going to conduct business and what you need to conduct it with.

If the owner allows it, try to get a brief walkthrough or tour of the house or area first so it can be drawn and observed to help the investigators match the stories with a visual reference. The layout will also become critical if you eventually do an onsite investigation. It will be used to plan out tests and experiments and it's essential that each investigator has their own layout as a reference. It's also advisable to get photographs of the rooms if allowable for reference as well, but ask for permission first!

Before getting too far in the interview process, or just before leaving for the evening, it would be advisable to discuss the release of information. I typically carry release forms (confidentiality as well as liability forms for when we are investigating) with me that explain that I will not release any information about this case to the public in any form without the owner's consent. I also have the owner sign one that says they will not do the same about our investigation without our consent. This may calm their fears or concerns that we are going to use their information for our gain, or ease our worries that they are out to use their story to write a book or gain media attention. Always cover your rear end in these cases when dealing with the public with the release of information as well as liability forms when conducting investigations on private property.

It is also advisable to use video or audio during the interview so you can have a record of what is said for review at a later date, again, get permission first. If they seem a bit awkward about the idea then do not do it. The more documentation you have about what you do the easier it will be to verify or dispute evidence, if you have nothing to verify it must automatically be disputed.

Conducting the actual interview should be controlled by you. When it starts out it will begin this way, but eventually the interviewee will begin to trail with their answers or get off topic. Your job is to control the interview by sticking to your questions and controlling what is being discussed to the best of your ability. While going through your interview you will come up with new questions. Don't be afraid to slow down to write these down or ask them right away.

Another phenomenon that may happen in a group setting is more than one witness talking at a time. At times this can be helpful since you will see how they interact with their answers or how they react to different information. Sometimes it can be distracting as one person will feed information or "control" what the other is thinking. This is of little help since we are looking for this individual's experiences and thoughts. If it is possible try to interview people separately at the same time, obviously in different rooms. This is a good tactic to employ to see how stories match up in cases where there are multiple witnesses to various events, just be sure to have two interviewers per witness.

Interviewing a witness with two investigators is an important strategy for a number of reasons. It gives one person the opportunity to focus on writing, while another can observe the witness for body language cues or if they look to another person in the room for answers, etc. It also allows for two people to interpret what is being said versus one so that there is a greater possibility that information is not lost during the interview. Other reasons include a quicker interview process and training for others to become better interviewers.

One variation of using two interviewers has one person asking questions and another writing down the answers. The person asking the questions should remain focused on the interviewee and watch how they answer the question (body language, looking away constantly) and should write down thoughts or feelings of the answers given as well as potential questions to ask based upon their answers. This method can create a one-on-one feeling with the other person writing the answers or information being off to the side and out of the conversation.

Another variation is that one person asks the questions as well as writes down the answers, the other person is an observer and merely writes down thoughts or body language cues during the interview. The former method may take longer and may at times take the focus off of the interviewee as the interviewer waits for the other to write down the answers. This is a good method if the person asking the questions is a better interviewer and the person observing is the better observer.

The latter is a better method overall. It is quicker, as well as easier for the client as there is only a focus on the interviewer and interviewee. There will be less focus on the observer as the questions and answers are being submitted by the same person and the observer may go several questions without writing much down at all and can even be across the room (seemingly doing something else, if the interviewee is the nervous type). The witness should also be thinking of questions to ask based upon answers given.

Despite which method is used, both interviewers should compare notes as quickly after the interview process as possible. Sometimes I have told the witnesses that we need a few minutes to compare notes outside or have done this informally by taking a break outside. Generally, you would do this after the interview/investigation process either on the ride home or at a location that night or the following day. The sooner the better as the information and questions are still fresh on your mind.

What are we looking for during the interview? The first thing we need to assume is that the events happening to the individuals are exactly what they perceived; we don't want to doubt that they observed something even if there is a logical explanation. We do want to be on the lookout or note possible logical explanations to explore during the interview process. Introduce these possible explanations to individual events slowly during the interview process. If they seem like a valid possibility be sure to note them for follow-up during an investigation. We also may note possible logical explanations during an initial walkthrough. Many times I will merely note these possibilities and will discuss them if the stories told may tie in with my possibility, either way test these theories with the investigation.

During the interview process we must keep our minds open for what we are looking for. Many factors may need to add up to determine a natural or unnatural explanation. Keep in mind these clues to narrowing our search for information.

- Is there any relation to the events and a particular location? Particular person? Time of day? Day of the week? Month? Year? Does anything repeat itself with the events every (or nearly every) time?
- Is there any frequency to the events? Has there been an increase or decrease in intensity? Has there been an increase or decrease in frequency?
- Is there any reason for anyone in the house to create these events? Are there family or personal problems? Stress that the person normally does not deal with? New things in their life? Drug abuse or other substance abuse clues? Past medical problems that may be a factor? (Epilepsy)
- Do the events hint to a ghost, haunting or a

poltergeist situation
-Has anyone researched the past history of the home or the property location?

Patterns are very important in the interviewing process. A pattern of answers or clues can tell us if the person is making things up or if someone may be the center of a poltergeist situation. Always look for consistency with the story and be weary of things added later on or differences in the story between two people (pending their perspective to the event).

In addition, we also must be aware of the environment (if we are in the area of the events) if anything should happen during the interview. Did something bother the interviewee or the "ghost"? Or was it merely something of coincidence? If there are specific events happening in the home, use this to your advantage even during the interviewing process. Again, it is suggested that the interview be recorded on video or at least audio.

Always know when to end your time in someone's house. If they seem impatient, frustrated or continuously look at their watch, offer to come back later. Always leave them with an idea of what will come next and always get back with them 24 hours after leaving the site whether you have come to a conclusion as to what to do next or not, they will be wondering.

All the clues may not be able to be put in place immediately and a time away from the location is usually necessary to process the information. It is best to meet up with the group of interviewers immediately upon leaving the location (and maybe bringing in others who were not present) to discuss things that you observed or felt about the situation. It helps if everyone arrives and departs together to help in this process (do not do this in the client's driveway!).

Treat any conversation as a group interview, record and take notes. Many findings are found outside of the location and when the interviewers are able to put their thoughts together. If it is not possible immediately following the interviews, each person should review their notes as soon as possible and write down any thoughts, questions or ideas to be expressed within the group or to the interviewee at a later date. All of the interviewees should gather within a few days of the interview to discuss their findings (they should compile them as they go through their own findings to note form for all to see). Write the questions and responses on paper and make copies for each person as well as maintain a separate master copy for the case records.

All notes should be kept for a master file which should contain records for all contact between any member of the group and the client. All tape (or video) recorded evidence should be kept secure and with the main file when the interviewer is finished processing it. Every note taken is important. The key is to keep everything and to keep everything organized and neat. If that means typing everything out, then do it! Proper record keeping could be the difference between making a discovery and making a fool out of yourself. In the long run all cases should be looked at to find correlations in findings or reactions or answers to particular types of questions. Proper and neat record keeping is essential for the current client's needs as well as our needs down the road if you are going to compile our information to research findings over time.

When the group has discussed the interview process at length they should determine whether to invoke further questions, an on site investigation of the areas, or to instruct them to keep documentation and let you know of any new developments. Let the client know of your intended plans and find out if they agree or wish to have an alternative next step. Be willing to compromise. Many times another interview process will be in order. This is where "feeling out" a case is important. If, when going along with questioning, you personally feel another visit will be necessary, try to establish that right away. Always let the client know of possible next steps in your intentions, they must be part of the plan. If you know further questioning will be in order then let them know and save an extended walk-through of the location for the follow-up interview process. Let the client know that extensive interviewing is critical in this situation as it is not possible to find answers with mere electronic tools or taking photographs or even bringing in a psychic or sensitive. The more information we can sift through the better chance we have of finding out the truth.

Chapter 3: Science of Investigation

The aspect of investigating on site is what most of us look forward to, just remember to do your interviewing and other background research before conducting an investigation. All of these things rely on each other to relate the information to the experiences to any data you may record.

When conducting the investigation be sure to plan it around the client as well as the investigators time frame. Be sure the atmosphere of the investigation is as close to "normal" as possible. Keep visitors and tagalongs of the owner and of the investigators out of the area. Anyone wandering around the location will render all of your evidence gathered as potentially tainted and not presentable as evidence.

When the client or you decide to conduct an investigation, be sure to have various tests designed around searching for logical clues. Re-enacting events may help you or the client realize logical explanations. Re-enacting events may also be a way to spur the "ghost" to making an appearance. The key is to try to reconstruct events, duplicate patterns, and recreate conditions of the events where they occurred. Induce controls (if applicable) slowly and gradually noting any changes in readings or feelings. Remember to stay relaxed, calm, and keep your body loose. Try not to let your nerves get in the way. Stay focused on the environment and the people around you.

Setting up experiments and areas to place equipment should be done in advance. Using your notes from the interviews, investigators should come up with an overall approach to how they will conduct the investigation. Establishing a timetable in advance will also give you an idea (as well as the client) how long the investigation will last. It will also ensure that everyone has a responsibility on site and that everyone will be on the same page as far as where to be and where not to be at various times.

The experiments and tests should be designed using not only the notes of the interviews but the floor plan drawn during the interview as well. The floor plans should have information notated about various objects within the house (plumbing, air and heating ducts, reflective surfaces if flash photography is used) depending upon the type of events occurring in each room (apparitional events, notate windows and reflective surfaces that may throw light). As each investigator should have their own floor plan as well as investigation time plan, they should use it to document their own evidence along the way (temperature, EMF baseline data to be compared with other investigators).

If there is to be EVP recordings set up in particular rooms or floors then investigators should not enter these rooms or even pass by if possible and should stay on the floor below. When using audio recording I use a "top-down" method, meaning I record from the top rooms while I investigate the lower ones before moving the recording equipment down. This eliminates potential creaking or footsteps from above; it does not eliminate the risk of talking coming from vents from lower levels. Be sure to test these out before setting up audio equipment if being left in a room by itself.

This brings up another important point: Documentation. Documentation should be an important part of the entire investigation process. No information should be ignored. If you sneeze, notate the time and location. If walking down a hallway, notate it. If you hear laughing, a car driving past the house, anything, notate it. I like to carry a micro cassette or digital recorder with me at all times so I can dictate what I am personally doing at all times as well as notate other things I hear throughout the area. Be sure to note times so that all data can be researched to ensure the possible contamination can be distinguished from potential evidence.

The experiments, tests or observations should be split into two categories; the logical and the paranormal. The logical should take priority and for your first on site investigation should comprise the majority of time spent investigating. Looking at each event separately is key here; you may be able to eliminate aspects of this case one by one. Be sure to demonstrate these findings to other investigators to get their input prior to giving this as a possible solution of one aspect the client.

With paranormal experiments you are attempting to create or observe spontaneous events from the ghost or haunting as well as attempt to record data to accompany these sightings. Remember, you should always think of yourself as a documenter, recorder and investigator, do not merely try to have your own experience in these situations. Observing an event alone does not give credence to the investigation, there may be many explanations for your observations, the goal is to have documentation backing up your observations (EVP, EMF, video, etc.).

If utilizing an EMF detector (gauss meter, magnetometer), be sure to have baseline readings done of that particular location prior to investigating or during to find locations and explanations for spike readings. If an event occurs during a spike this is a great documentation piece since one event backs up another. Be sure to revisit this exact spot later to verify the spike was random.

With the recreation of events, it is logical as well as productive to have the client be part of the experiment. This is logical since the events are occurring around this particular person and you will definitely have a higher chance of recording events with this person present. Granted, many people may not wish to participate with this, but if they are willing be sure to capitalize on this opportunity.

Another attempt at observation comes at taunting or "baiting" the apparition into appearing. This attempt comes at various levels from being mean to merely asking questions. Many investigators use this approach when using EVP by asking questions aloud to hopefully be answered on the recorder. Some investigators may be mean toward the apparition. I do not recommend this approach for any type of investigation as it will certainly not make anything easier for anyone.

Remember, an apparition is a reflection of a once living person. The personality displayed through the events will be very similar to that of the person when they were still living. If the events are construed as mean it does not justify being this way toward the apparition, though it will always pay to be direct in dealing with any type of apparition.

You may also try indirect evidence such as video

taping a room or location without an investigator present. This may be in a child's room at night or other location with or without a person present. Since ghosts are linked to human experience it makes sense to have the experiment correlate with a living person present. This type of experiment may also include chalk-lining items that purportedly move (though video of this would be far more productive) or other methods of investigation that do not include the investigator being present in the room or possibly at the location. The only limits you should have on your experiments are those placed by the homeowner.

There are multiple ways to attempt to record data for apparitional cases. Re-enacting events or recreating the settings gives you the most opportunity for successful documentation of evidence. Again, the key is to first attempt to find logical explanations for individual events that have happened to the homeowner (no matter how mundane the event and no matter how convincing the case is toward a ghost being present). Elimination of various events lets you focus on the ones that can not be explained for further focus. Do not expect to come to any type of conclusion right away or on your first investigation to a location. It may take several follow-ups to record anything worthwhile. Just remember that the goal should be to help the client, many times this may mean not having the experience you may desire, but your personal goals should be outweighed by the needs of the client.

Other than searching out for logical explanations, possible interactions and subsequent recording of data, we need to be on the lookout to fully determine what we are dealing with. The interview process may help you determine better if you are dealing with an apparition or haunting. The investigation may prove one way or the other based upon your observations and data. If it is a haunting you will have to rely on the interview evidence to determine a trigger or timeframe for these events to be later verified (hopefully) by observation and backup with tools.

Once you have finished for the night and pack up your gear, be sure to have some sort of post investigation talk with the group as soon as possible. Just like after the interview session, this may be done on the drive home or after stopping somewhere on the way home. This exchange of information may benefit the outcome of individual pieces of evidence and may provide answers that may pop up while you are reviewing your evidence. After reviewing your evidence be sure to meet up as a group to discuss your findings prior to meeting up with the homeowner, but always be sure to maintain contact with them during that time.

Chapter 4: Conducting a Hunt

This chapter is written for the group that is conducting a ghost hunt or investigation where there may not be a pressing need to find an answer to an event. The other distinction from an investigation is that the location is one where there are no first hand witnesses to current events. These places might include cemeteries, abandoned buildings or existing places of business that have a reputation or stories about being haunted.

A hunt is a great way to harden your nerves in the field of paranormal investigation as well as develop methods of investigation and working with your group as a team. I highly recommend conducting rudimentary investigations with new teams to help the team become more cohesive as well as to help ease your fear of being in these situations and develop your observational skills. It may also help identify those who may not be able to handle the environment of paranormal investigation before getting into a client situation.

The most important thing for your group to do is to thoroughly research this area before arriving and conducting an investigation. Are the stories about this place possible or true? Is there any way to speak to anyone who may have witnessed events at this location? Attempt to find reasons to potentially verify the possibility of these events or to discount their possible validity. Showing up at a site with instruments to gather data is quite elementary in makeup as well as for potential evidence gathering. If you have no reason to verify ghost activity your potential evidence will have no reason to provide anything of legitimacy.

The second most important thing is to be sure to get permission to enter this area during whatever time it is you wish to investigate. Even cemeteries will have people who will look after these sites and it would be helpful for you to know if there is a funeral scheduled the day you decide to show up (that would not be a good thing).

During a hunt you are concentrating solely on your environment for experiences or anything out of the ordinary to occur. Be sure not to expect things to happen too dearly as many can be easily fooled by an explainable event. If you do observe or hear something be sure to investigate that event further for a possible logical explanation.

Just as with an investigation, be sure to plan out what types of observations and experiments in advance with the group. Be sure that everything is documented during EVP, photographs or any other sources of data collection. The key with a hunt would be to tie an experience together with a form of data collection (EMF, EVP, photo, etc.).

Chapter 5: The Follow-up

You have reviewed your information from your case, now what? Did you find anything of interest? If yes, you'll want to present this information to the group first (as stated earlier) to determine if something happening during the investigation that could provide a logical explanation of events. If no, you'll want to present this to the client to determine your next course of action.

Typically, you may need more than one investigation to find any evidence to support the client or to find reasons to doubt individual events. Again, the most important thing about these investigations is what the client wants in the end. If all they desire is for evidence to be found then I would question their motives. Typically, clients just want the events to stop and will look to you for help in this area. If you can not help the client at this point do not be afraid to tell them so, just be sure to find an avenue for them to explore next (psychic investigator, another group, counselor, etc.).

Usually, the investigator will not observe any events and when the client seeks help the events may cease altogether for some odd reason. If the client begins to have confidence of their situation it may also help ease and eventually end the events. No matter what the client needs to have the feeling that they control this situation and to communicate that with the apparition.

A key to being a continued success in this field is to continue to follow up with clients no matter what the outcome. If the events seem to terminate the client typically does not contact you again. It is wise to check in from time to time on clients of past investigations. Admittedly, I have not always done this and I realize now how I feel like I have not fulfilled my obligation to these clients. We all become busy in our work and our next investigation, but always check up on those in which you have helped in the past to not only see if the events have stopped or started back up, but to ensure they have been able to cope with the situation and have been able to move on in their lives.

Chapter 6: The Tools

The focus of groups in recent times has been the tools associated with hunting ghosts. There are no tools specifically designed for observing or detecting ghosts. This technology has been adapted from other sources to attempt to record the residual energy from ghosts or hauntings. There have been some tools that have been constructed specifically for this field, but contain too many variables to be considered useful for investigating.

Some tools have been used in combination with each other. Examples of which are A.R.C.A.D.I.A. (which I have been fortunate to see in action) and M.E.S.A. which are essentially tools linked together via a laptop computer to gather data from each device simultaneously.

The use of tools has confused many ghost hunters and paranormal investigators as to the role this equipment. These tools are not a substitute for interviewing or researching a site beforehand. An anomalous reading or recording of a tool does not mean something paranormal was observed via the tool or recording device. In order for a reading or recording to be viewed as potentially paranormal there must be an event observed by someone which coincides with the data or recording.

Know how to use your equipment inside and out or do not bother bringing it with you. Be ready and able to explain what each piece of equipment is used for and what it may help to find with the investigation to the client and other witnesses. Be honest and truthful about the information given.

Before arriving to an investigation, make sure you have all of your equipment and check or change all batteries. Make sure you will have enough batteries, tapes (camcorder or tape recorder) or film (if using a 35 mm) to complete the investigation time frame. Do not load film or tapes until you arrive at the location, and only do so in front of a witness or member of the location to verify authenticity of equipment records (label each audio or video tape as well as the film canister before loading to ensure proper documentation). This process has nothing to do with the ghosts (as some websites suggest) it merely insures that the evidence collecting methods are un-tampered with in the beginning. Always include the date, time, investigator, and client name on all information.

The most important tool you can bring to a site is an open mind. Not just open to the world of ghosts, but to the world of reality. Always use these tools to first find a logical explanation before assuming there is a paranormal one. Here's a list of the basic physical tools involved.

- ✓ ***Notebooks, Pens, Pencils, Highlighters*** - Anything to take written record of everything you do on site or during interviews. Use various writing utensils for specific jobs, remember- always bring extras!
- ✓ ***Pre-drawn layout of Grounds or Site***-

This may be drawn or taken from outside sources or be done on site before actual investigation takes place. With this goes **graph paper** and **tracing paper**. Tracing paper can be put over the graph paper design of the house or room if copies are not available. This helps when you are away from the site to get a visual. Use it to mark events and other items in rooms or hallways (reflective surfaces if photographed, etc.). This should be copied and distributed to every member on the on-site investigation team.

✓ *Camera* - Not to snap photos of ghosts, but to document the layout for future reference. Use it to photograph areas with readings that suggest possible disturbance. If using a film camera; load cameras at the site and bring plenty of film. 400 speed film is recommended (the higher the speed the grainier the photo especially when enlarged). There are theories about using higher speed film, but nothing conclusive. Digital cameras have mostly replaced the film cameras and have many advantages over them. One very simple advantage is being able to take quality pictures in low light (indoors) without use of a flash. This cuts down on reflections (and would eliminate many orb shots if people would do this) without hurting detail. Film photographs were traditionally studied by their negatives for flaws, digital processing eliminates flaws created by chemicals used to transfer negatives to photos, but still may be subject to other flaws and do not have a physical negative to study. Digital photos can be studied easily by utilizing digital photo software.

- ✓ ***Camcorder*** - Use this in the same fashion as described for the camera. This gives you sound and moving picture to reference to, giving you better leverage in any type of investigation. Do not forget extra tapes or discs! These can also be left on site to document things while you are away. The best recording equipment would be CCTV with night vision and 24 hour recording DVR.
- ✓ ***Flashlights*** - Note the plural. Bring more than one flashlight (even during the day) and plenty of batteries. A red lens attachment is good for "night vision" or helping your eyes stay adjusted to the dark (this is a great help with perception). There are some windup flashlights on the market which may be good for a backup but are a pain to use on a consistent basis. *Hint: try to match up battery types for the equipment you intend to buy. The most flexible of these items is the flashlight. If you recorder uses AA, your EMF detector uses AA, find a flashlight that uses AA. This saves time, money and weight.*
- ✓ ***Tape Recorder*** - These include a shoebox type, micro-cassette or digital. An external Omni-directional microphone is preferred. Do not limit these devices to EVP recording, use

these to tape witnesses (get permission) and to record your investigation for your own personal records. Don't forget to bring extra tapes and batteries. If you're looking to buy a digital recorder, be sure to buy one with software or at least a USB connection so that you can use it on audio software as well as record it to other media.

- ✓ ***Electronic sensing devices*-** An EMF detector (electromagnetic field detector, magnetometer or gauss-meter), thermal scanner, thermal imaging camera, etc. The EMF detector is the most popular (and probably the most misunderstood) tool of paranormal investigation. It seems to be the "must have" tool, although the tools themselves may be more readily designed to help eliminate potential events than register them. The most important thing about using EMF detectors is knowing why or why not to use them. These tools are **not ghost detecting devices**; they measure the fields or energy that the apparition or haunting has affected. These devices are used to back up witness testimony or actual events, used by themselves do not offer any evidence to a paranormal event. Temp sensors are used to notate fluctuations in temperature as observed by witnesses. Be sure these devices are used to search for explanations first (windows, doorways or other draft sources) before settling for a paranormal explanation. Also, be certain that these recordings coincide with an event or other tool reading or the data may merely be a random event.

✓ ***First aid kit*-** This is an obvious tool for any outdoor or night time investigation.

Part IV: Resources

Chapter one: The Scientific Method

A major theme of psychology and other sciences that sets them apart from ghost hunting and paranormal investigation (not necessarily parapsychology) is that they are empirical in nature. That is, the study of these sciences has been set by observation, experiments and practical experience. It is not based on theory, speculation, armchair theorem or uncritical common sense. Therefore, ghost hunting or paranormal investigation is not really a science, until we have documented, studied, theorized and disseminated findings within (and outside) the field repeatedly.

I talk about using science in investigations and I am not talking about merely using the popular tools to do so. The application of science is not simply using your tools or merely knowing how to use them, it's what you do with them and what is else is happening that is important as well as the conclusions and follow-ups you do with the information you gather. Here is a taste of science that you need to satisfy the hunger of scientists, the public and media to help bring our field into legitimacy as well as make what you do in the field translate from evidence to answers.

The Scientific Approach

There are three sets of interrelated goals; measurement and description, understanding and prediction, and application and control.

Measurement and Description- Before a scientist can explain why the world works in a certain way; they need to describe *how* it works. Science's commitment to observation usually requires that an investigator figures out a way to measure the phenomenon under study. The goal here is to develop measurement techniques that make it possible to describe behavior clearly and precisely. The attempt is made by using gadgets such as EMF detectors, thermal imaging cameras, etc. The problem lies in the fact that ghost hunters are only concerned with the "what" instead of the "how". The "how" is how the devices are detecting what they are detecting as well as how they know it is an apparition they are recording. This is also difficult, if not impossible, since most of what they record with these devices is spontaneous in nature as with all Psi phenomena.

Understanding and Prediction- Scientists believe that they understand events when they can explain the reasons for their occurrence. To evaluate their understanding, scientists make and test predictions about relationships between variables. This seems like an easy one, but we have little understanding of what is going on with ghosts. We have been able to predict certain behaviors, but we have yet to learn the causes that lead to these behaviors. Psi phenomena is the same, not yet knowing how (or where in the brain) it exists nor can we predict when it will occur.

Application and Control- Ultimately, most scientists hope that the information they gather will be of some practical value in helping solve everyday problems. Once people understand a phenomenon, they often can exert more control over it. . When we begin to understand how ghosts come into existence or devise a practical means to communicate with them the World as we know it will become a different place. The same holds true if we are able to utilize ESP or Psychokinesis on a daily basis at any degree.

Steps in a Scientific Investigation

1. Formulate a Testable Hypothesis

The first step is to translate a general idea into a testable hypothesis. A hypothesis is a tentative statement about the relationship between two or more variables. Hypotheses are generally expressed as predictions. They spell out how changes in one variable will be related to changes in another variable. To be testable, scientific hypotheses must be formulated precisely, and the variables under study must be clearly defined. Researchers achieve these clear formulations by providing operational definitions of the relevant variables. An operational definition describes the actions or operations that will be made to measure or control a variable. Operational definitions establish precisely what is meant by each variable in the context of a study. Most ghost groups come up with theories, which are based upon unproven ideas or speculation of how events may hold an answer. A theory is merely a guess and has no application toward science, but can help lead to a hypothesis.

2. Select the Research Method and Design the Study.

The second step in a scientific investigation is to figure out how to put the hypothesis to an empirical test. The research method chosen depends to a large degree on the nature of the question under study. The various methods: experiments, case studies, surveys, naturalistic observation, each have advantages and disadvantages. The researcher has to ponder the pros and cons and then select the strategy that appears to be the most appropriate and practical. Once researchers have chosen a general method, they must make detailed plans for executing their study.

3. Collect the Data

According to their plans, researchers obtain their samples of subjects and conduct their study. Psychologists use a variety of data collection techniques, which are procedures for making empirical observations and measurements. Commonly used techniques include direct observation, questionnaires, interviews, psychological tests, physiological recordings, and examination of archival records. These methods are broken down below. Collecting research data often takes an enormous amount of time and work.

Direct observation - Observers are trained to watch and record behavior as objectively and precisely as possible. They may use some instrumentation, such as a stopwatch or video recorder.

Questionnaire - Subjects are administered a series of written questions designed to obtain information about attitudes, opinions, and specific aspects of their behavior.

Interview - A face-to-face dialogue is conducted to obtain information about specific aspects of a subject's behavior.

Psychological test - Subjects are administered a standardized measure to obtain a sample of their behavior. Tests are usually used to assess mental abilities or personality traits.

Physiological recording - An instrument is used to monitor and record a specific physiological process in a subject. Examples include measures of blood pressure, heart rate, muscle tension, and brain activity.

Examination of archival records - The researcher analyzes existing institutional records (the archives), such as census, economic, medical, legal, educational, and business records.

4. Analyze the Data and Draw Conclusions

The observations made in a study are usually converted into numbers, which constitute the raw data of the study. Researchers use statistics to analyze their data and to decide whether their hypotheses have been supported. Thus, statistics play an essential role in the scientific enterprise.

6. Report the Findings

Scientific progress can be achieved only if

researchers share their findings with one another and with the general public. Therefore, the final step in a scientific investigation is to write up a concise summary of the study and its findings. Typically, researchers prepare a report that is delivered to a journal for publication.

The process of publishing scientific studies allows other experts to evaluate and critique new research findings. Sometimes this process of critical evaluation discloses flaws in a study. If the flaws are serious enough, the results may be discounted or discarded. This evaluation process is a major strength of the scientific approach, because it gradually weeds out erroneous findings. For this reason, the scientific enterprise is sometimes characterized as "self-correcting".

This is why it is critical for ghost hunting and paranormal investigation groups to share and compare data. We are stuck making the same guesses over and over from one group to the next until the data is put out there for everyone to evaluate. Each group feels that they alone will produce a piece of ground-breaking evidence that will set the World on its ear, this is a belief founded in misunderstanding of how the scientific process operates. Groups must work together building upon work to come up with answers. It is possible that one group may eventually hold the key but this group will be one that uses the scientific approach from work that eventually will be confirmed or denied by others.

Advantages/Disadvantages of the Scientific Approach

The Scientific approach offers clarity and precision. Common-sense notions tend to be vague and ambiguous. The major advantage of the scientific approach is its relative intolerance of error. While possibly not proving anything beyond argument, the scientific approach does tend to yield more accurate and dependable information than casual analyses and armchair speculation do. Knowledge of scientific data can thus provide a useful benchmark against which to judge claims and information from other kinds of sources.

The major disadvantage of the scientific approach (especially in the case of ghost research) is that experiments are often artificial. Experiments require great control over proceedings and researchers must construct simple contrived situations to their hypothesis experimentally. It is practically impossible to simulate the environment of a haunted location in a laboratory setting, this is why there is no experimentation within the study of the paranormal- not only can we not duplicate this environment we could never possibly control it.

We must rely solely on descriptive research methods. These methods are used when the variables can not be manipulated. In other words, these methods can not be used to describe cause-and-effect relationships between variables. Though this could come with time and understanding and after the use of the descriptive research. Descriptive methods permit investigators only to describe patterns of behavior and discover links or associations between variables. This is where Parapsychology has been stuck for over 100 years. Once variables are introduced the results usually seem to become inconclusive.

Descriptive research cannot demonstrate conclusively that two variables are causally related.

Descriptive research methods include:

Naturalistic Observation

A researcher engages in careful, usually prolonged, observation of behavior without intervening directly with the subjects. The problems with this approach are twofold. First, it is nearly impossible to observe ghost activity for a prolonged period of time, especially when dealing with a specific case. This lack of observation time usually proves the information gathered inconclusive. Secondly, it is nearly impossible to observe the ghost behavior without becoming directly involved with the subjects. We try hard to gather as much as possible and to go in to a location at the last possible second, but with this you risk not being able to observe any activity yourself.

Once you are part of the environment you have changed the variables and altered the environment in which the events occur.

Case studies

These are in-depth investigation of an individual subject. Data is collected for individual cases and compared to that of other cases to arrive at a common explanation. The major problem with this approach is that they are highly subjective. The information from several sources must be knit together in an impressionistic way. During this process one may focus on information that fits with their expectations, which usually reflect their theoretical slant. Thus, it is relatively easy for investigators to see what they expect to see in case study research.

Surveys

Researchers use questionnaires or interviews to gather information about specific aspects of subjects' behavior. Surveys are often used to obtain information on aspects of behavior that is difficult to observe directly. Surveys also make it relatively easy to collect data on attitudes and opinions from large samples of subjects. The major problem with surveys is that they depend of self-report data. Intentional deception and wishful thinking can distort subjects' verbal reports about their behavior.

Scientific research is a more reliable source of information than casual observation or popular belief.

However, it would be wrong to conclude that all published research is free of errors. Scientists are fallible human beings, and flawed studies do make their way into the body of scientific literature. This is why replication of a study (or observation) is important. Replication of a study may lead to contradicting results. Some inconsistency in results is to be expected, given science's commitment to replication. Fortunately, one of the strengths of the empirical approach is that scientists work to reconcile or explain conflicting results. In fact, scientific advances often emerge out of efforts to explain contradictory findings. This is very important to keep in mind as we collect data and continually observe findings in the field. We must not always be too quick in search of the answer, or the truth may elude us. Looking at conflicting evidence is very healthy and may lead us to the answers.

Flaws in evaluation of research

A sample is the collection of subjects selected for observation in an empirical study. In contrast, the population is the much larger collection of animals or people (from which the sample is drawn) that researchers want to generalize about. Sampling bias exists when a sample is not representative of the population from which it was drawn. We must be careful to not draw conclusions until we are able to deal with a diverse array of the public, which will give us a fair sample of the overall population which is encountering these occurrences.

Placebo effects occur when subjects' expectations lead them to experience some change even though they receive empty, fake, or ineffectual treatment. Placebo, for our concern, may happen if we give them information on the subject. They may conform their observations on the new information given to them or alter what has happened in the past or jump to quick conclusions about natural experiences. The overall effect of the thought of a ghost is interacting with them causes some to distort previous experiences. We must be careful with what information we give them and at what time we give it.

Social desirability bias is a tendency to give socially approved answers to questions about oneself. This could also include conforming your observations by what is popularly known to be ghost activity. Example; someone feels a draft in their house and assumes it is a ghost, they may lump other unrelated experiences with it to draw the conclusion or convince others based on the current social trends of paranormal activity.

Experimenter bias occurs when a researcher's expectations or preferences about the outcome of a study influence the results obtained. This is a common problem with ghost research on many different levels. The first that comes to mind is that we (like some who experience ghosts) jump to conclusions based on bits of information obtained during the case. We must learn to look at each piece of evidence as separate and not lump everything together immediately and assume every clue adds another piece of the puzzle and help confirms a ghost. Another problem lies with the popular orb photographs. In this we have a tendency to draw our conclusions from what we see or believe not what we can prove or study. We must not try to "see what we want to see" and look for viable evidence to deny any rational or natural explanations first and foremost.

We must take what the history of science has given us and use it to our advantage, it can only help us confirm or deny what we set out to find.

Information from this chapter gathered from "Psychology Themes and Variations, second edition", Wayne Weiten (Brooks/Cole Publishing 1989).

Chapter 2: Recommended Books

These books are non-fiction, in other words they are not ordinary ghost stories. They cover the reality behind the myths and uncover parts of the unknown. Most books on ghosts can be found in your local library under 133.1 under the Dewey Decimal System. Some of these books are no longer in print or you may have to special order from your local major bookstore. I have found many of these in used book stores as well. This is by no means a complete list of what is out there, it is only a sample. These are books I own or have read or can truly say they have value to the field. Many of the authors shown here have other books relevant to the subject.

Ghosts, Hauntings and Poltergeists

Danelek, J. Allan. (2006). *The Case for Ghosts: An Objective Look at the Paranormal.* Woodbury, Minnesota. Llewellyn Publications.

Denning, Hazel M. (1996). *Hauntings! Real-Life Encounters with Troubled Spirits.* New York, NY. Barnes & Noble Books.

Holzer, Hans (2005, 1965). *Ghosts I've Met.* New York, NY. Barnes & Noble Books / Aspera Ad Astra, Inc.

Holzer, Hans (1997). *Ghosts: True Encounters with the World Beyond.* New York, NY. Aspera Ad Astra, Inc.

Iverson, Jeffrey. (1992). *In Search of the Dead: A Scientific Investigation of Evidence for Life after Death.* San Francisco. Harper.

Kachuba, John B. (2004). *Ghosthunting Ohio (The Haunted Heartland Series).* Cincinnati. Emmis Books.

Mackenzie, Andrew. (1982). *Hauntings and Apparitions: An Investigation of the Evidence*. London. Paladin Books.

Ogden, Tom. (1999). *The Complete Idiot's Guide to Ghosts and Hauntings*. Indianapolis, Indiana. Alpha Books.

Peach, Emily. (1991). *Things That Go Bump in the Night*. Wellingborough, Northhamptonshire, Great Britain. The Aquarian Press.

Rogo, D. Scott. (1979). *The Poltergeist Experience*. New York. Taplinger Publishing Co.

Rogo, D. Scott. (1986). *Life after Death: The Case for Survival of Bodily Death*. Wellingborough, Northhamptonshire, Great Britain. The Aquarian Press.

Roll, William G. (1976). *The Poltergeist*. Metuchen, NJ. The Scarecrow Press.

Spencer, John and Anne. (1997). *The Poltergeist Phenomenon*. London, England. Headline Book Publishing.
Underwood, Peter. (1994). *Ghosts and How to See Them*. London. Anaya Publishers Ltd.

Paranormal Investigation

Auerbach, Loyd. (2004). *Ghost Hunting: How to Investigate*

the Paranormal. Oakland: Ronin Publishing.

Auerbach, Loyd. (2005). *A Paranormal Casebook: Ghost Hunting in the New Millenium*. Dallas, Texas. Atriad Press LLC.

Baker, Robert A. and Nickell, Joe. (1992). *Missing Pieces: How to Investigate Ghosts, UFOs, Psychics and other Mysteries*. Buffalo, NY. Prometheus Books.

Taylor, Troy. (2001). *Ghost Hunter's Guidebook*. Chicago. Whitechapel Productions.

Underwood, Peter. (1986). *The Ghost Hunter's Guide*. London. Javelin Books.

Warren, Joshua P. (2003). *How to Hunt Ghosts: A Practical Guide*. New York. Fireside.

Parapsychology (and general psychic abilities)

Auerbach, Loyd. (1986). *E.S.P., Hauntings and Poltergeists: A Parapsychologists Handbook*. New York: Warner Books.

Auerbach, Loyd. (1991). *Psychic Dreaming: A Parapsychologist's Handbook*. New York. Warner Books.

Auerbach, Loyd. (1993). *Reincarnation, Channeling and Possession: A Parapsychologist's Handbook*. New York.

Warner Books.

Auerbach, Loyd. (1996). *Mind Over Matter.* New York. Kensington.

Berger, Arthur S. and Joyce. (1991). *The Encyclopedia of Parapsychology and Psychical Research.* New York. Paragon House.

Braude, Stephen E. (1991). *The Limits of Influence: Psychokinesis and the Philosophy of Science.* New York. Temple University Press.

Broughton, Richard S. (1991). *Parapsychology; The Controversial Science.* New York: Ballantine Books.

Broughton, Richard S. and Roll, William G. (1995). *Psychic Connections: A Journey into the Mysterious World of Psi.* New York. Delacorte Press.

Browne, Silvia. (2000). *The Other Side and Back: A Psychic's Guide to Our World and Beyond.* New York. Signet.

Edge, Hoyt L., et al. (1986). *Foundations of Parapsychology: Exploring the Boundaries of Human Capacity.* London, England. Routledge & Kegan Paul.

Edward, John. (2000). *One Last Time: A Psychic Medium Speaks to Those We Have Loved and Lost.* Berkeley Publishing Group.

Guiley, Rosemary Ellen. (1991). *Harper's Encyclopedia of Mystical and Paranormal Experience.* San Francisco. Harper Books.

Irwin, H.J. (1994). *An Introduction to Parapsychology 2nd. Ed.* Jefferson, NC. McFarland & Company.

Kripper, Stanley (Ed.). (1994). *Advances in Parapsychological Research.* Jefferson, NC. McFarland & Company.

Kurtz, Pau (Ed.). (1985). *A Skeptic's Handbook of Parapsychology.* Buffalo, NY. Prometheus Books.

Radin, Dean I. (1997). *The Conscious Universe: The Scientific Truth of Psychic Phenomena.* New York. HarperCollins.

Rhine, Louisa E. (1981). *The Invisible Picture.* Jefferson, NC. McFarland & Co.

Rogo, D. Scott. (1986). *Mind over Matter: The Case for Psychokinesis.* Wellingborough, Northhamptonshire, Great Britain. The Aquarian Press.

Schmeidler, Gertrude R. (1988). *Parapsychology and Psychology: Matches and Mismatches.* Jefferson, NC. McFarland & Company.

White, Rhea. (1990). *Parapsychology: New Sources of*

Information, 1973-1989. Metuchen, NY. The Scarecrow Press.

Wills-Brandon, Carla. (2000). *One Last Hug Before I Go: The Mystery and Meaning of Deathbed Visions.* Health Communications.

Zollschan, George K., Schumaker, John F., Walsh, Greg F. (1989). *Exploring the Paranormal: Perpectives on Belief and Experience.* New York. Avery Publishing.

Developing Psychic Abilities

Hewitt, William W. (1996). *Psychic Development for Beginners: An Easy Guide to Releasing and Developing your Psychic Abilities.* St. Paul, MN. Llewellyn Publications.

Holzer, Hans. (1997). *Are You Psychic? Unlocking the Power Within.* New York, NY. Avery.

Konstantinos. (2001). *Contact the Other Side.* St. Paul, Minnesota. Llewellyn Publications.

Mishlove, Jeffrey. (1988). *PSI Developement Systems.* New York. Ballantine Books.

Sanders, Pete A. (1989). *You are Psychic!* New York. Fawcett Columbine.

Scott, Gini Graham, PH.D. (1991). *Shamanism and Personal Mastery.* St Paul, Minnesota. Paragon House.

Weil, Andrew. (1995). *Spontaneous Healing*. New York. Alfred A. Knopf.

Miscellaneous

Ackerman, Diane. (1990). *A Natural History of the Senses*. New York. Random House.

Blum, Deborah. (2006). *Ghost Hunters: William James and the Search for Scientific Proof of Life After Death*. New York. Penguin Books.

Dennett, Daniel C. (1991). *Consciousness Explained*. Boston. Little, Brown and Co.

Murphy, Michael. (1992). *The Future of the Body: Explorations Into the Further Evolution of Human Nature*. Los Angeles. Jeremy P. Tarcher.

Ormstein, Robert. (1991). *The Evolution of Consciousness*. New York. Prentice-Hall Press.

Penrose, Roger. (1994). *Shadows of the Mind: A Search for the Missing Science of Consciousness*. Oxford, England. Oxford University Press.

Stapp, Henry P. (1993). *Mind, Matter and Quantum Mechanics*. Berlin. Springer Verlag.

Chapter 3: Terminology

In this chapter I am including terminology discussed in this book as well as basic terms of use as a beginning investigator and popular terminology used by Parapsychologists. To see my full list of terminology, please visit the glossary section at ghosthelp.net/glossary.html.

Agent - (1) Person who attempts to communicate information to another in an ESP experiment. (2) The subject in a psychokinesis experiment. (3) Person who is the focus of poltergeist activity.
Apparition - The visual (or other senses) appearance of a person whose physical body is not present. Typically apparitions display intelligence and communication abilities which are related to how they were during life. To some this word merely describes seeing a ghostly figure.
Apport / Asport - An apport is a solid object that seemingly appears from nowhere in the presence of a medium. Asport is any object the 'spirits' or medium makes disappear or teleports to another location.
Astral body - The body a person seems to occupy during an out-of-body experience.
Astral plane - A world some people believe exists above the physical world.

Astral projection - An out-of-body experience.

Astrology - A theory and practice which attempts to identify the ways in which astronomical events are correlated with events on earth.

Aura - A field that some psychics see surrounding the living body.

Automatic writing - Writing without being aware of the contents, as when a medium apparently transcribes written messages from disembodied spirits.

Automatism - Any unconscious and spontaneous muscular movement caused by 'the spirits'. (Automatic writing).

Autoscopy - Seeing one's 'double', or looking back at one's own body from a position outside the body (OBE).

Bilocation - Being (or appearing to be) in two different places at the same time (similar to autoscopy).

Case study - An in-depth investigation of an individual subject.

Channeling - The process by which a medium apparently allows a spirit to communicate through his or her person.

Clairaudience - Auditory form of ESP (compare with Clairvoyance).

Clairsentience - Physical sensations (or smell) form of ESP. Sometimes used as a general term for clairvoyance and clairaudience.

Clairvoyance - A subset of ESP. The viewing of distant scenes not apparent to the eye, may appear externally - either replacing the normal visual scene (visions) or being incorporated into it (as could be the case with apparitions) - or internally, in the form of mental imagery and intuition.

Cold reading - A technique using a series of general statements, questions, and answers that allows fake mediums, mind-readers, and magicians to obtain previously unknown information about a person. (Reader has no prior knowledge).

Collective apparition - An unusual type of 'ghost' sighting in which more than one person sees the same phenomenon.

Control - In experimental parapsychology a procedure undertaken in order to ensure that the experiment is conducted in a standard fashion and so that results are not unduly influenced by extraneous factors.

Control Group - A group of people whose performance is compared with that of experimental subjects.

Crisis apparition - An apparition seen when the subject is at the point of death or is the victim of a serious illness or injury.

Cross-correspondences - Interrelated bits of information received from 'the spirit world' by different mediums at different times and locations. The communications must be **joined** together to form a complete message from 'the spirit(s)'.

Decline Effect - A decrease in performance on a psi test when the test is repeated.

Déjà vu - The feeling of having experienced something before.

Dice Test - Experimental techniques for investigating

psychokinesis, in which a subject attempts to influence the fall of dice.

Direct voice phenomenon (DVP) - A 'spirit' voice, spoken directly to sitters at a séance. The sound usually seems to come from a point near the medium, or through a spirit horn or trumpet, but not from the mouth of the medium.

DMILS - Direct Mental Interaction with Living Systems. Used to denote instances where one person is attempting to influence a distant biological system, usually the physiology of another person. As it is unclear whether this represents an influence (PK), a case of ESP on the part of the influence, or an opportunistic selection process (see DAT), the term 'interaction' has been adopted.

Doppelganger - A mirror image or double of a person.

Double Blind - An experimental procedure in which neither the subject nor experimenter is aware of key features of the experiment.

Electromagnetic Field Detector (EMF, or gauss meter, magnetometer) - A device which measures electric, magnetic, radio or microwave fields.

Empathy - Rarely used in modern parapsychology, the popular usage of this term refers to a low-level form of telepathy wherein the empath appears to be aware of the emotional state of a distant person. An empath may also be able to "broadcast" emotions to others.

Empiricism - The premise that knowledge should be acquired through observation.

ESP - Extrasensory perception. (Receptive psychic) The ability to gain knowledge through means other than the five physical senses or logical inference.
Electronic voice phenomenon (EVP) - The capture of 'spirit' voices on magnetic tape or digital media as an audio recording. Many times, no sound is heard while the tape is recording. It's only upon playback that the harsh, hushed voices can be heard.
Evidence- Something that gives a sign of the existence or truth of something, or that helps somebody to come to a particular conclusion.
Experiment - A test carried out under controlled conditions.
Experimental Group - A group of subjects who undergo a specific experimental procedure. Often results from this group are compared with those of a control group.
Experimental Parapsychology - Parapsychology research involving experimental methods rather than survey techniques or the investigation of spontaneous cases.
Experimenter - The person who conducts the experiment.
Experimenter Effect - Influence that the experimenter's personality or behavior may have on the results of an experiment.
False Awakening - An experience in which a person believes he or she has woken up, but actually is still dreaming.
Forced choice experiment - An experiment in which the subject is forced to choose among an assortment

of possible targets, such as the five ESP cards.

Free response experiment - An experiment in which the subject knows only the general nature of the target - for instance, that it is a picture - but not anything else.

Ganzfield experiment - An experiment where input from the outside world is reduced by placing halved ping-pong balls over the eyes and by masking external sounds (covering subject's ears with headphones and playing white noise). A state of mild sensory deprivation.

General Extrasensory Perception (GESP) - ESP in which it is unclear whether the results are due to clairvoyance, telepathy, precognition or retrocognition.

Ghost - A form of apparition, usually the visual appearance of a deceased human's 'spirit soul' or that of a crisis apparition.

Ghost hunt / Ghost investigation - A ghost hunt is an informal attempt to simply sight or record a 'ghost' in a location similar to others known to be haunted. A ghost investigation, on the other hand, is a carefully controlled research project, set up to record paranormal activity, usually at a location known, or presumed to be haunted.

Goat - A subject in an experiment who does not believe in the ability for which he or she is being tested.

Hallucination - Perception of sights, sounds, etc., that are not actually present. Ghosts, as we define them, are not hallucinations, because they have a real, external cause.

Haunting - Recurrent sounds of human activity, sightings of apparitions, and other psychic phenomena, in a location when no one is there physically. This definition may differ depending upon group's perception of the basic terms of ghost, haunting and apparition. At times haunting as a descriptor word with prefix attached (residual, true, etc.)

Hot Reading - A reading given in which prior knowledge of the sitter has been obtained, often using devious or fraudulent means.

Hypnosis - State like sleep in which the subject acts only on external suggestion.

Illusion - A distorted perception of objects or events causing a discrepancy between what is perceived and what is reality. (Sometimes confused with hallucination)

Incline Effect - An increase in performance on a psi test when the test is repeated.

Intuition - The non-paranormal ability to grasp the elements of a situation or to draw conclusions about complex events in ways that go beyond a purely rational or intellectual analysis.

Kirlian Photography - A photographic method involving high frequency electric current, discovered by S.D. & V. Kirlian in the Soviet Union. Kirlian photographs often show colored halos or "auras" surrounding objects.

Laying on of hands - A process by which certain healers profess to be able to heal patients by touch.

Levitation - The lifting of physical objects by

psychokinesis (PK).

Life Review - Flashback memories of the whole of a person's life often associated with the near-death experience.

Magnetometer (EMF detector, gaussmeter) - A device to measure the presence of a magnetic field as well as its strength, direction, and fluctuation. Paranormal researchers use the device in an attempt to detect a ghost's magnetic or energy aura.

Mean Chance Expectation (MCE) - The most likely chance score in a psi test.

Medium - A person who professes to be able to communicate with spirits.

Medium (direct voice) - A trance medium who apparently acts as a transmitter for the voices of disembodied spirits.

Medium (materialization) - A medium who seems to be able to give physical form to the deceased from a substance called "ectoplasm".

Medium (physical) - A medium who is the center of moving objects and other physical incidents supposedly caused by spirits.

Mesmerism - The induction of a sleep or trance state, discovered during the work of Friedrich Anton Mesmer, from whose name the word is derived. *Also known as hypnotism.*

Mist - A photographed anomaly (not seen at time of photo) that appears as a 'blanket' of light. Theory suggests that this is the appearance of a 'ghost' or 'spirit' of the dead. As with other photographed anomalies there are environmental issues that are of concern to the validity of their existence (moisture, reflection, dirty lens, etc.). There has been no substantial proof that these are, or are related in any way, to 'ghosts' or paranormal behavior.

NDE - Near-death experience - the out-of-body and other experiences people report having when they are close to death. Events within NDE include: an OBE, life review, a tunnel experience (drifting in darkness), encounters with guides (or angels), seeing dead relatives or friends, a moment of decision (or being told) to turn back.

OBE - Out-of-body experience - the experience that the self is in a different location than the physical body.

Objective apparitions - Apparitions or phenomena that appear independent of our minds, thoughts, or feelings.

Orb - A photographed (not seen at time of photo) or visual anomaly that, in theory, represents an ongoing 'spirit' of a deceased person. It appears as a ball of light and may occasionally seem to be moving. This is a highly controversial subject since there are many reasonable circumstances that identify this as environmental (dust, rain, snow, dirty lens, insects, reflection, lens flare etc.). There has been no substantial proof that the balls of light are associated with 'ghosts', the dead or any paranormal behavior.

Ouija Board - A board pre-printed with letters, numerals, and words used by mediums to receive spirit communications. Usually a planchatte (palm-sized triangular platform) is employed to spell out words or point out numbers or letters. A game version of the Ouija board was mass-marketed as OUIJA by Parker Brothers in 1966 and is currently distributed by Hasbro.

Paranormal - Above or outside the natural order of things as presently understood.

Parapsychology - The branch of science that studies psychic phenomena (term coined by J.B. Rhine).

Percipient - A person who sees (i.e., perceives) an apparition or ghost.

Phenomenology - An approach to research that aims to describe and clarify a person's own experience and understanding of an event or phenomenon.

Poltergeist - A German word meaning 'noisy or rowdy ghost' (see also RSPK).

Process Research - Research that aims to investigate factors affecting psi.

Proof - Conclusive evidence: evidence or an argument that serves to establish a fact or the truth of something.

Proof Research - Research that aims to demonstrate the existence of psi.

Psychical Research - Term coined in the late 19th century to refer to the scientific study of the paranormal. Now largely superseded by 'parapsychology'.

PK - Psychokinesis - (expressive psychic) the power of the mind to affect matter without physical contact.

PK (bio) - Psychokinetic influence of biological systems e.g. changing the physiological activity of a living system (see DMILS).

PK (deliberate) - Psychokinesis that occurs as a result of conscious effort by the person causing it.
PK (macro) - The effect of psychokinesis on objects in general.
PK (micro) - The effect of psychokinesis on random events such as random event generators (REGs).
PK (spontaneous) - Psychokinesis that occurs without conscious effort by the person who causes it.
PK (time-displaced) - The concept of psychokinesis going backward in time to affect events that have already taken place.
Place memory - Information about past events that apparently is stored in the physical environment.
Precognition - The ability to predict things beyond present knowledge.
Psi - A letter in the Greek alphabet that denotes psychic phenomena.
Psi hitting - A test performance significantly higher than expected by chance.
Psi missing - A test performance significantly lower than expected by chance.
Psyche - The Greek word for "self", "mind", or "soul".
Psychic - A person with above average ESP abilities.
Psychic healing - A mode of healing affected by the psychic abilities of the healer.
Psychic surgery - The supposed ability to paranormally perform invasive surgery using no conventional medical tools.
Psychometry - ESP of events associated with inanimate objects.

Qualitative Method - A research method involving the collection of non-quantitative data (e.g., observations, interviews, subjective reports, case studies).

Quantitative Method - A research method involving the collection and statistical analysis of numerical data.

Radio voice phenomenon (RVP) - Receiving the voice of a deceased human being over a regular radio.

Remote viewing - (1) Another term for clairvoyance. (2) An ESP procedure in which a percipient attempts to become aware psychically of the experience of an agent who is at a distant, unknown target location.

Repressed psychokinetic energy - A theoretical psychic force produced, usually unconsciously, by an individual undergoing physical or mental trauma. When released, the power causes paranormal occurrences such as poltergeist activity.

Response - An action made by a subject in an experiment.

Response bias - Tendency of a subject to prefer particular responses.

Retroactive Psychokinesis - Paranormal influence that an agent can have on an experiment after it has been completed.

Retrocognition - A 'time warp' in which one finds themself in the past, seeing or experiencing events of which they had no prior knowledge.

RSPK - Recurrent spontaneous psychokinesis. A possible cause of apparent poltergeist activity.

Skeptic - A person inclined to discount the reality of

the paranormal and to be critical of parapsychological research. Generally seeks rational or scientific explanations for the phenomenon studied by parapsychologists.

Scrying - A term used to cover a wide range of divination techniques which parapsychology would tend to classify as types of ESP. Most scrying techniques involve some degree of fixation on a surface with a clear optical depth (crystal ball, a pool of ink or deep water) or on an area which shows random patterns (flames in a fire, smoke), the idea being that subconscious information available to the scrying will be manifested in their interpretation of the imagery or random patterns they see.

Séance - A group of people who gather in an effort to communicate with the dead.

Shaman - A 'wizard' in tribal societies who is an intermediary between the living, the dead, and the gods.

Sheep - A subject in an experiment who believes in the ability for which he or she is being tested.

Spirit photography - A spirit photograph captures the image of a ghost on film. Many of these are supposedly intended as a mere portrait of a living human being, but when the film is developed, an ethereal ghostly face or figure can be seen hovering near the subject. This may also incorporate orbs, vortexes, and mists to some degree.

Spirit theater - A term used by modern-day magicians to describe shows, acts, or tricks in which ghosts or other spirit activity are apparently produced.

Spiritualism - A belief system that 'spirits' of the dead can (and do) communicate with living humans in the material world. (Usually through an intermediary known as a medium).

Subjective apparitions - Apparitions or phenomena that are hallucinations created by our minds.

Supernatural - Something that exists or occurs through some means other than any known force in nature. As opposed to paranormal, the term 'supernatural' often connotes divine or demonic intervention.

Statistics - Mathematical techniques for analyzing and interpreting data.

Survey - A method of data collection that involves interviewing (or giving questionnaires to) a representative and often large group of people.

Target object - In ESP, the object or event the subject attempts to perceive; in PK, the object or event the subject attempts to influence.

Telekinesis - Paranormal movement of objects.

Telepathy - The direct passing of information from one mind to another.

Teleportation - A kind of paranormal transportation in which an object is moved from one distinct location to another, often through a solid object such as a wall.

Thought form - An apparition produced by the power of the human mind.

Trance - A sleeplike state in which there is a change of consciousness.

Trial - In psi tests, a single attempt to demonstrate paranormal ability (e.g., one attempt to guess a card or

one attempt to influence the fall of the dice).
Vortex (vortice) - A photographed anomaly that appears as a funnel or rope-like image (sometimes creating a shadow) that is not seen at the time of the photograph that supposedly represents a 'ghost'. Other theories include; a collection of orbs, a 'gateway' to where orbs originate or travel to or a wormhole in time-space. No substantial evidence has been found for any of these theories.
White noise - A hiss-like sound, formed by compiling all audible frequencies (used in Ganzfield experiments).
Zener Cards - Set of 25 cards (5 each of circle, square, Greek cross, five-pointed star, three wavy lines) designed by the perceptual psychologist Karl Zener for use in card-guessing tests of ESP. (also known as ESP cards).
This by no means is a complete dictionary of terminology. This is meant to provide you with pertinent words to aid in the basic understanding of parapsychology and the ghost hunting world.

Information for this glossary taken from <u>Michael Daniels, PhD.</u>, **Psychic Connections: A Journey Into the Mysterious World of Psi** *by Lois Duncan and William Roll, PhD.(Bantam Doubleday Dell Books, 1995),* **The Complete Idiot's Guide to Ghosts and Hauntings** *by Tom Ogden (Alpha Books 1999),* **Psychology Themes and Variations second edition** *Wayne Weiten (Brooks/Cole Publishing 1989)*

Chapter 4: Further Information

I have not included website links in this book as most of this information is easily available and since so much of this information changes so frequently. There are links to further information for much of what I have discussed in this book on my website at ghosthelp.net). From the links area you will find group links, parapsychology information (books and journals), paranormal news, equipment links and more.

Ghosthelp.net is nothing more than a gateway to the path of information, the site is meant for education and admittedly provides you with only a taste as to what this field can bring to fill your mind. I urge you to read as many websites as possible and to critically review the information given (is it fact or opinion and how is it really presented to the reader?).

I am in the process of writing a companion book to this one which will dig further into the investigation aspect. It will be based upon a tool I wrote for my group to help them understand what I do when I receive e-mails from contacts. It will be written in a running dialogue fashion that will follow a scenario of a case from start to finish. It will hopefully help prove to be a valuable tool when reading potential case e-mail as well as provide you with an idea of what you may be dealing with. Look for *Betty's Ghost: A Guide to Paranormal Investigation*, hopefully coming soon.

Additionally, this companion book will also have additional resources to the ones I have provided here. I will share various links that I use on a daily and weekly basis. I will also share other resources I have gathered or created along the way.

If you have any questions, comments or desire further information about what I have written, feel free to contact me at opin2u@gmail.com.

Finally, I would like to thank Dan Bautz , the webmaster and podcast host of The Grand Dark Conspiracy website (www.granddarkconspiracy.com) for having me as a guest on a recent podcast from his site. I look forward to sharing more information with him and his audience in the future.

www.ingramcontent.com/pod-product-compliance
Lightning Source LLC
Chambersburg PA
CBHW022152080426
42734CB00006B/399